Pornography: How to Get It Off the Internet Internationally

Sara Johann
J.D. M.A. M.S.

Pornography: How to Get It Off the Internet Internationally

Copyright 2019 by Sara Johann, Independent Publisher

London UK and Wisconsin USA 2019

Cover Art by Sara Johann

All rights reserved. No part of this book may be reproduced in any form, except for brief quotation in reviews, without the written permission of the author.

Contact Author Sara Johann at saraljohann@gmail.com. **Learn more about her at** https://www.linkedin.com/in/sara-johann-499aa324/

Novels by Sara Johann

A Masquerade of Murder

(Cassandra) St. George Slays the Dragon

The Wisdom Conspiracy, a Vatican Thriller

The Genome Dilemma

The Missing Messiah

Strangers (Writing as Nicola Rossi)

Johann authored an encyclopedia against pornography citing thousands of professional sources and also authored numerous laws books against abuse of persons.

Table of Contents

Introduction

Chapter One: Reasons for Regulating Pornography

Chapter Two: What Is Pornography and How Can We Define It?

Chapter Three: Understanding the Obligations of States Under International Human Rights Treaties, Universal Jurisdiction, Norms, Jus Cogens, Obligations Erga Omnes, Customary International Law, and Due Diligence

Chapter Four: To What Extent Do Existing International Treaties and Agencies Regulate Pornography?

Chapter Five: Is Or Can Torture Pornography Be Regulated By International Law?

Chapter Six: Shutting Down the Pornography Industry: Proposals for Change

Conclusion

Bibliography

Introduction

The goal of this book is to demonstrate that there is an obligation on the part of states, founded in international human rights law or other international law, to prohibit or outlaw the production, distribution, dissemination, possession, and use of child pornography, and adult image based sexual abuse, violent, torture, extreme, and nonconsensual pornography worldwide. If such an obligation exists, actions should be taken by states to shut down the pornography industry.

Existing international human rights, criminal laws and customary international law will be examined to determine whether an obligation exists. Proposals will be made for how to increase the effectiveness of existing legal remedies for fighting Internet pornography. Ideas will be offered regarding potential new laws and strategies. These include creation of an international cybercrime treaty, specifically adding pornography as human rights violation under various human rights treaties, proposing states act to shut down and block pornography sites on the Internet, creating enforcement mechanisms for human rights treaties, and potentially creating an international human rights court.

Chapter One discusses reasons to regulate pornography. Chapter Two presents several different approaches to defining pornography. Chapter Three details the obligations of states under international human rights treaties, universal jurisdiction, international norms, *jus cogens*, obligations *erga omnes*, customary international law, and due diligence. Chapter Four covers the extent to which current international treaties, and committees regulate pornography and the obligations of states under such treaties. Chapter Five focuses on whether or not certain types of pornography can be considered torture under international law. Chapter Six makes suggestions regarding how to shut down the pornography industry and makes proposals for change (as mentioned above). A Conclusion is then presented.

The biggest problem with tackling pornography is that, as Shytov notes, individual nations cannot successfully regulate pornography content which flows globally, and there is no specific international agreement banning all types of pornography on the Internet.[1] There are old treaties which

---

[1] Alexander Shytov, 'Indecency on the Internet and International Law,' [2005] 13(2) Int'l J. of Law and Inform. Tech., 260-280, 263

apparently are no longer enforced regarding the circulation of obscene publications, he notes, listing The Agreement for the Suppression of the Circulation of Obscene Publications (1910), amended by a Protocol in 1949, and the International Convention for the Suppression and the Circulation and Traffic in Obscene Publications (1923) (amended in 1947).[2] While there are weaknesses in the treaties regarding defining obscene materials and indecency, he believes these treaties could be applied to the Internet, noting, however, that many nations have not signed these treaties although many European nations have, as have the U.S. and Russia, with only 60 of 191 UN nations as treaty members.[3]

Salomon believes that the universal principle of respecting and observing human rights which began with the UN charter includes political and civic rights [later codified in ICCPR], as well as socio-economic rights [later codified in ICSCR]. The theory of human rights entitles every person to live in conditions of dignity.[4] Such human rights are considered

---

[2] *Ibid.*, 264
[3] *Ibid.*
[4] Margot E Salomon, *Global Responsibility for Human Rights: World Poverty and the Development of International Law* (OUP 2010, 2007), 161

to have universality and apply to all people everywhere. The International Court of Justice has repeatedly held that states are obligated to "observe basic human rights as a matter of custom," she states.[5]

We represent that the right to human dignity under international human rights law includes the right to be free from sexual violence and abuse, which the pornography we wish to ban consists of and demonstrates. Pornography is an international human rights issue because it violates human rights and human dignity, including in ways which can be interpreted to be prohibited under international human rights norms and under various international treaties involving children, torture, women, discrimination, privacy, crimes against humanity, and more. As I demonstrate in this paper, it is also an international issue because it is primarily disseminated through use of the Internet to and from numerous different countries. It should be considered torture and a crime against humanity. Hornle and Kremnitzer agree that "pornographic images that show rape and other violent sexual acts are incompatible with human dignity" because the

---

[5]*Ibid.*, 165

victim is being used as an object and humiliated.⁶ They posit that this is an objective value that could justify prohibiting production and sale of such pornography.⁷

Two major international human rights are at issue in pornography cases, namely, the right to privacy and the right to freedom of expression, Suzor, Seignior, and Singleton explain. When international treaties are involved, legitimate limits may be found as long as three conditions are met, they state:

> First, the restriction must be provided for by law. Second, it must be necessary for the 'respect of the rights or reputations of others', 'national security', 'public order' or 'public health or morals.' Third, it must meet the 'strict tests of necessity and proportionality.' Necessity requires that the objective could not be met in a way that does not restrict the right to freedom of expression. Proportionality requires that restrictions are 'appropriate to achieve their protective function' and 'proportionate to

---

⁶Tatjana Hornle and Mordechai Kremnitzer, 'Human Dignity As A Protected Interest In Criminal Law,' [2011] 44 Israel L. Rev. 143, 157

⁷*Ibid.*,167

the interest to be protected.' [Here it could be argued that sharing nonconsensual intimate images violates the right to privacy of victims and 'appropriate limitation can be said to be necessary for the 'respect of the rights and reputations of others.'] [Sources omitted][8]

There is, however, another major human rights interest at stake in pornography cases, and that is, as Paul Johnson, notes, the right to be free from degrading treatment (such as that contained in Art. 3 of the ECHR).[9] The international human right of persons not to be subjected to sexual abuse and to not have their abuse photographed and distributed in any way, including in cyberspace, must take precedence over any alleged free speech right.

---

[8] Nicolas Suzor, Bryony Seignior, and Jennifer Singleton, 'Non-Consensual Porn and the Responsibilities of Online Intermediaries,' [2017] 40 Melbourne U. L. R. 1057, 1072
[9] Paul Johnson, 'Pornography and the European Convention on Human Rights,' [2014] 1(3) Porn Studies, 299, 301

Chapter One: Reasons for Regulating Pornography

We find four major reasons for banning/criminalizing pornography:

1. Child pornography consists of images of sexual abuse of real children, which is something that international society firmly does not condone. Much adult pornography also consists of actual sexual abuse of real women and men, which also cannot be condoned. Child pornography is a target of law enforcement efforts across the world because of the cycle of child pornography which has been described by O'Brien:

> (1) child pornography is shown to a child for 'educational purposes'; (2) an attempt is made to convince a child that explicit sex is acceptable, even desirable; (3) the child is convinced that other children are sexually active and that such conduct is okay; (4) child pornography desensitizes the child, lowering the child's inhibitions; (5) some of these sessions progress to sexual activity involving the child; (6) photographs or films are taken of the sexual activity; and (7) this

new material is used to attract and seduce yet more child victims.[10]

Child pornography production and use has grown greatly due to the Internet, digital photography developments, easy access, partial anonymity, the difficulty of policing an international problem, and the limited risk of being detected, Akdeniz notes.[11] I would add that, since the availability of Tor, The Onion Router, enabling child pornographers and their customers to be anonymous on the Internet, child pornography has become an even greater global problem. As of 2009, the child pornography industry had a value of up to 20 billion dollars a year according to the Special Rapporteur on the Sale of Children, Child Prostitution and Child Pornography, Najat M'jid Malla.[12]

---

[10] S. O'Brien, *Child Pornography*, 2nd edn [1992] Dubuque, IA: Kendall Hunt, cited in Akdeniz, *supra,* 5

[11] Yaman Akdeniz, *Internet Child Pornography and the Law National and International Responses* [2008, 2009] Farnham, Surrey: Ashgate Publishing, Ltd., 8

[12] Warren Binford, 'A Global Survey of Country Efforts to Ensure Compensation for Child Pornography Victims,' [2015] 13(1) Ohio State J. of Crim. L. 37, 38, citing Najat M'jid Malla (Special Rapporteur on the Sale of Children, Child Prostitution and Child Pornography), Promotion and

Bursztein, et al., 2019, detailed the extent of the problem (with CSAI standing for Child Sexual Abuse Images) noting that the National Center for Missing and Exploited Children handled 23.4M incidents of CSAI from 1998–2017 with 40 percent of the incidents being from 2017 alone. They state: "Protecting against CSAI requires coordinated, global action. Ten years ago, 70% of CSAI reports reflected abuse in the Americas. Today, 68% of reports relate to abuse in Asia, 19% the Americas, 6% Europe, and 7% Africa."[13] Noting that the proliferation of CSAI videos is due to cell phone abilities, sharing of such videos went from under 1000 reports a month in 2013 to over 2 million a month, they explain that this

---

Protection of All Human Rights, Civil, Political, Economic, Social and Cultural Rights, Including the Right to Development, par 44, 80, Human Rights Council, U.N. Doc. A/HRC12/23 (July 13, 2009).

[13] Elie Bursztein, Travis Bright, Einat Clarke, Michelle DeLaune, David M. Elifff, Nick Hsu, Lindsey Olson, John Shehan, Madhukar Thakur, Kurt Thomas, 'Rethinking the Detection of Child Sexual Abuse Imagery on the Internet' [2019] In Proceedings of the 2019 World Wide Web Conference (WWW '19), May 13–17, 2019, San Francisco, CA, USA. ACM, New York, NY, USA, 7 pages. https://doi.org/10.1145/3308558.3313482, 1-2

interferes with the ability of law enforcement and society to combat such images.[14]

2. There is substantial social science and law enforcement data and research available showing at a minimum, a correlation, and at a maximum, causation between use of pornography and sexual abuse of real women, children and men. It can also be shown that publication of and repeated sharing of such images of actual sexual abuse of real people causes those who were abused and photographed to suffer emotional and/or psychological injuries. Both of these aspects are what is referred to as a harm related or health related justification. We will not be documenting harms in this short article but did so at length thirty years ago in a prior law book.[15] Fuller describes the harms:

> Women are coerced and brutalized into making pornography, women are forced to act out these violent scenes in their bedrooms, women in the workplace are

---

[14] Bursztein, et al., 5
[15] Sara Johann, *Sourcebook On Pornography* [1989] Lexington, MA: Lexington Books

subjected to it, and women are the victims of the increased sexual violence it causes.[16]

3. Morality and decency. Banning pornography is often justified on the grounds of public morality. Such grounds, in my view, are sufficient to justify such a ban on image based sexual abuse, nonconsensual pornography, extreme and violent pornography, revenge pornography, and child pornography. Shytov describes adult pornography as threatening traditional cultures and their concepts of decency, finding an international obligation "to protect world cultures and cultural diversity" as grounds to suppress adult pornography, meaning that proving individual harm is not necessary.[17] One issue raised regarding the morality grounds is "whether a society has the right to enforce its morality in the absence of proven harm."[18]

4. Pornography is an organized crime industry. See, for reference, the Final Report of

---

[16] Elizabeth Kirby Fuller, 'Holding Producers and Distributors Liable for the Harms of Sexually Violent Pornography through Tort Law,' [1994] 5 Fordham Intell. Prop. Media & Ent. L. J. 125, 128-129

[17] Shytov, 260

[18] Susan Easton, 'Criminalizing the Possession of Extreme Pornography: Sword of Shield?' [2011] 75 JCL 391-413, 396

the Attorney General's Commission on Pornography, 1986, and Johann, *Sourcebook*, 1989. MacKinnon states that, despite trafficking of pornography by legitimate corporations, the industry remains "an organized crime industry built on force, some physical, some not."[19] Dimoulas, Karagianni, Patroni, and Tsogkas [2018] state that child pornography is the second "most profitable globalized illegal activity" after drug trafficking.[20] Hidden Internet services such as Tor Network, Dark Web, Freenet, and Cloud computing contribute to this problem.[21]

---

[19] Catharine A. MacKinnon, 'Pornography as Trafficking,' [2005] 26(4) Mich. J. of Int'l Law 993, 995. See her fn. 9 for sources.

[20] Vasilis Dimoulas, Maria Karagianni, Eugenia Patroni, and Lampros Tsogkas, 'Child Pornography In A Cloud Era,' [2018] THEMIS Competition 2018,Semi Final A- International Cooperation in Criminal Matters, National School of Judges, 1

[21] *Ibid.,* 1

Chapter Two: What Is Pornography and How Can We Define It?

The absence of a common internationally accepted definition of pornography/obscenity makes it difficult to shut down the pornography industry and deal with this issue on a global level.[22] We recommend that a common definition of pornography be adopted internationally and reflected in each state's national laws.

First, we want to avoid definitions which are vague or overbroad. Helen Longino defined pornography as material "that explicitly represents or describes degrading or abusive sexual behavior 'so as to endorse and/or recommend the behavior described.'"[23] This definition is overbroad and vague. A potential defendant cannot be certain what is prohibited contrary to the rule of law and international human rights due process concepts.

---

[22] Shytov, 260

[23] Claudia Giunta, 'International Human Rights Standards on Sexual Violence against Women as They Apply to Pornography,' [1997] *LLM Theses and Essays*. 196. https://digitalcommons.law.uga.edu/stu_llm/196
Accessed Internet 19 July 2019, 14-15, quoting Helen E. Longino, 'Pornography, Oppression and Freedom: A Closer Look,' in *Take Back the Night: Women on Pornography* [1980] New York: William Morrow and Company, Inc., 42

Second, many definitions of pornography include two main elements. The Attorney General's Commission on Pornography defined pornographic in 1986: "[T]he material is predominantly sexually explicit and intended primarily for the purpose of sexual arousal."[24] The Optional Protocol to the international Convention on the Rights of the Child described below requires that a depiction of the sexual parts of a child be shown primarily for sexual purposes to be actionable.

A. Differentiating Erotica from Pornography

Society probably does not want children exposed to images of sexually explicit conduct. Regarding adults---do we want to outlaw *all* depictions of sexual acts or only certain types of depictions? For example, don't some paintings and statues and photographs of nude persons, or even of adult persons engaged in sexual acts have artistic value? Does the context of the depiction matter? If the photograph is of a person which was meant to remain private, it should remain private.

---

[24] Attorney General's Commission on Pornography, *Final Report* (Washington, D.C.: United States Department of Justice), 228-229

We are not arguing that all sexually explicit images of adults should be prohibited by international law. Freedom from Sexual Violence described how erotica differs from pornography by defining erotica as:

> [T]he presentation of mutually pleasurable sexual expression between consenting individuals which involves positive and affectionate human sexual interaction and desires.[25]

B. Defining Child Pornography/Child Sexual Abuse Images

Let us turn to child pornography as a starting point of international agreement on what should be outlawed regarding children.

The first point of potential debate is the age of the child. Can all nations agree to define "child" for purposes of child pornography laws, as anyone under the age of 18?

The Optional Protocol to the Convention of the Rights of the Child on the Sale of Children, Child Prostitution and Child Pornography was passed in 2000 to implement the purposes of

---

[25] Freedom from Sexual Violence [1985], *Violent Pornography: What It Is and Who It Hurts*, (Milwaukee, WI), 3

the CRC and to impose a duty on states to protect children from such exploitation. Child pornography is defined in Art. 2. as "any representation, by whatever means, of a child engaged in real or simulated explicit sexual activities or the representation of the sexual parts of a child primarily for sexual purposes."[26]

The United States Department of Justice states that child pornography "is a form of child sexual exploitation." It states that, under federal law, child pornography (also called child sexual abuse images, or CSAI) is "any visual depiction of sexually explicit conduct involving a minor (persons less than 18 years old)."[27] The DOJ also explains that for an image to be sexually explicit, it does not have to be of a child "engaging in sexual activity" but that a picture of a naked child can be illegal " if it is sufficiently sexually suggestive."[28] This definition seems very similar to the CRC Optional Protocol described above.

---

[26] *Ibid.*
[27] United States Department of Justice, https://www.justice.gov/criminal-ceos/child-pornography, Accessed, Internet, 10 August 2019
[28] United States Department of Justice, https://www.justice.gov/criminal-ceos/citizens-guide-us-federal-law-child-pornography, Accessed, Internet, 10 August 2019

To avoid problems of vagueness or overbreadth, laws regulating child pornography should also define what sexually explicit conduct is.

C. Obscenity Law Definitions

Many nations have laws criminalizing obscenity production and dissemination. For example, obscenity law in the U.S. requires that works must depict or describe sexual conduct which is specifically defined under the relevant state law and that the law must be a non-national/state offense. The key case is <u>Miller v. California</u>, 413 U.S. 15, 34 (1973) which added that the offense "must be limited to works which, taken as a whole, appeal to the prurient interest in sex, which portray sexual conduct in a patently offensive way, and which, taken as a whole, do not have serious literary, artistic, political, or scientific value." Noting that the *Miller* case is ineffective due to widely differing obscenity laws, the General Counsel for the Citizens for Decency Through Law supported a ban on all commercially distributed hard-core pornography with exceptions for legitimate use such as medical or educational purposes.[29] We

---

[29] Johann, *Sourcebook*, 6

agree that obscenity laws should be replaced with laws banning hard-core pornography, based on specified content, taking a judge or jury's opinion regarding what is moral or obscene or offensive out of the equation and making certain that offenders can identify precisely what materials are against the criminal law.

D. Extreme and Violent Pornography and Image Based Sexual Abuse

This article focuses on child pornography, adult extreme and violent pornography, image based sexual abuse, and nonconsensual pornography. Thus, such pornography must also be defined.

The UK made possession of extreme pornography a crime as of January 2009. Under Sec. 63 of the Criminal Justice and Immigration Act of 2008, the prosecution must prove that the image is pornographic and extreme ("grossly offensive, disgusting, or otherwise of obscene character") and portrays any of the extreme acts listed in 63(7) in a realistic and explicit manner.[30] 63(3) defines pornography:

> "An image is "pornographic" if it is of such a nature that it must reasonably be assumed to have been produced solely or principally for the purpose of sexual arousal."
>
> Sub. 7 states in relevant part: (7)An image falls within this subsection if it portrays, in an explicit and realistic way, any of the following—(a)an act which threatens a person's life, (b)an act which results, or is likely to result, in serious injury to a person's anus, breasts or genitals, (c)an act which involves sexual interference with a human corpse, or (d)a person performing an act of intercourse or oral sex with an animal (whether dead or alive),and a reasonable person looking at the image would think that any such person or animal was real. (7A) An image falls within this subsection if it portrays, in an explicit and realistic way, either of

---

[30] The Crown Prosecution Service, 'The Code for Crown Prosecutors: Legal Guidance, Extreme Pornography,' Accessed Internet 11 June 2019 at https://www.cps.gov.uk/legal-guidance/extreme-pornography

the following—(a)an act which involves the non-consensual penetration of a person's vagina, anus or mouth by another with the other person's penis, or (b)an act which involves the non-consensual sexual penetration of a person's vagina or anus by another with a part of the other person's body or anything else, and a reasonable person looking at the image would think that the persons were real. (7B) For the purposes of subsection (7A)—(a)penetration is a continuing act from entry to withdrawal; (b) "vagina" includes vulva."[31]

In 2015, extreme images of "non-consensual penetration and rape" were added to the definition of extreme pornography. On a positive note, this law was a major development in the arena of criminalizing pornography because it made it a crime to *possess adult* extreme *pornography*. A 2005 paper by the UK Home Office gave reasons for such a law including breaking up the supply and demand for such material "'which we

---

[31] Criminal Justice and Immigration Act 2008, 2008 c. 4, Part 5, Pornography, etc., Section 63, Accessed Internet 11 June 2019 at http://www.legislation.gov.uk/ukpga/2008/4/section/63

consider may encourage or reinforce interest in violent and aberrant sexual activity.'"[32] It also opposed such material because it "causes and celebrates suffering, pain and degradation, and the right to harm others is not protected by the free-speech principle," in Easton's words.[33]

How can we define "nonconsensual pornography?" Some call this "revenge porn." Many U.S. states have enacted laws against it. Donohue defines non-consensual pornography as "a brand of cyber harassment in which the violence and invasion involves posting nude or sexually explicit images without the consent of the person in the image."[34] I believe the concept of "nonconsensual" must also include pornography that results from photographed rapes, child molestation, child sexual abuse, and adult sexual abuse. Any sexually explicit photo or film of a person, whether adult or child, taken and/or shared without their consent would be covered under such a law.

---

[32] Easton, 394, citing Home Office, *Consultation: on the Possession of Extreme Pornographic Material: Summary of Responses and Next Steps* (Home Office/NOMS 2006) para. 14.
[33] Easton, 398
[34] Donohue, 254

E. Pornography Defined As Subordination of and Discrimination Against Women and Gender-Based Violence

In the 1980's, Andrea Dworkin and Catherine MacKinnon proposed an ordinance in Minneapolis, MN, USA to enable female pornography victims to recover damages in civil court. As a legislative drafting attorney, I brought the issue to the forefront in a similar proposal before the Wisconsin legislature in 1985 and expanded upon it in my encyclopedia against pornography in 1989.[35] An international human rights approach to this manner of regulating pornography can be justified because of the focus on torture and other cruel and inhuman treatment, on sexual violence, on gender-based violence against women, and on dehumanization and degradation. Dworkin and MacKinnon defined pornography this way:

> 'Pornography' means the graphic sexually explicit subordination of women through pictures and/or words that also includes one or more of the following: (a)

---

[35] Sara Johann, *Sourcebook On Pornography* [1989] Lexington, MA: Lexington Books

women are presented dehumanized as sexual objects, things, or commodities; or (b) women are presented as sexual objects who enjoy humiliation or pain; or (c) women are presented as sexual objects experiencing sexual pleasure in rape, incest, or other sexual assault; or (d) women are presented as sexual objects tied up, cut up or mutilated or bruised or physically hurt; or (e) women are presented in postures or positions of sexual submission, servility, or display; or (f) women's body parts---including but not limited to vaginas, breasts, or buttocks---are exhibited such that women are reduced to those parts; or (g) women are presented as being penetrated by objects or animals; or (h) women are presented in scenarios of degradation, humiliation, injury, torture, shown as filthy or inferior, bleeding, bruised, or hurt in a context that makes these conditions sexual.[36]

I do not believe that the ability to recover for damages due to being depicted in pornography

---

[36] Andrea Dworkin and Catherine A. MacKinnon, *Pornography And Civil Rights: A New Day for Women's Equality* [1988] 138-139

should be limited to women because men and children can be depicted in similar ways. I agree that pornography far more often depicts females in such a manner and is a form of sex discrimination (disproportionately impacting women), and encourages sex discrimination, sexual violence against females, and gender-based violence.

F. Definition Conclusion

In creating a definition of pornography for an international law, the hard-core/extreme nature of the pornography should be key, and certain criteria should be included, using portions of various approaches detailed above. Any exposure of children (under age 18) to sexually explicit or sexually suggestive materials should be prohibited. Concerning adult pornography: First, the images must be sexually explicit or, at a minimum, include exposure of a person's breast, vagina, penis or anus. Second, a means should be found to allow erotic art/erotica, and legitimate sex education or medical materials. Third, where child pornography is concerned any images which are sexually explicit or which feature breast, vagina, penis or anus or which is sexually suggestive should be covered under the law. Fourth, any nonconsensual images should be included in the prohibitions even if they are not extreme or violent. Fifth, the law should cover persons of all sexes. Sixth, the categories of images described in the MacKinnon-Dworkin definition above should be included and expanded to cover all persons, not just women, even though we recognize that such pornography primarily features sexual violence against and degradation of women, disproportionately affects women, and is therefore sex discrimination under international law. Seventh, the activities mentioned in the extreme pornography law from the UK cited above, including the additional coverage of rape and sexual assault pornography, should be covered in the definition. Eighth, real or imagined consent to sexual abuse depicted in the material should not be a defense. Definitions referring to obscenity or morality, which are not objective criteria, must be excluded from the law. What is covered by this definition must be described sufficiently for potential violators to be able to tell what is made criminally or civilly actionable under the law to comply with human rights to due process and the rule of law required by treaties and norms.

Chapter Three: Understanding the Obligations of States Under International Human Rights Treaties, Universal Jurisdiction, Norms, Jus Cogens, Obligations Erga Omnes, Customary International Law, and Due Diligence[37]

We will argue that many international treaties and agreements exist, detailed below, which can be understood as placing obligations on states to regulate child pornography and the types of adult pornography which concern us because they involve acts of torture, rape, sexual abuse, inhuman and cruel treatment, violence toward women, and sex discrimination toward real women and encourage other women to be treated in a similar fashion. We believe that, when a state signs and ratifies such treaties, they are under a positive obligation to take action to regulate pornography and to cooperate with other nations in doing so under the international law

---

[37] Parts of the *jus cogens* section are reprinted with permission from Sara Johann's summative essay at the City Law School, London, class in International Human Rights, 2019.

principles of *Jus Cogens,* Obligations *Erga Omnes,* international human rights norms, customary international law, and/or due diligence. Studying individual states and whether they are or are not meeting their obligations regarding regulating pornography is beyond the scope of this article.

A. Universal Jurisdiction

Langer explains that:

> Under universal jurisdiction, any state may prosecute a crime without having any territorial, national or national-interest link with the crime when the crime was committed.[38]

It is critical for human rights advocates to understand that, without the availability of universal jurisdiction over atrocity crimes (such as genocide, war crimes, crimes of aggression, and crimes against humanity) *only* the United Nations has jurisdiction over these core international crimes.[39] It has, from time to time, created ad hoc tribunals to regulate such acts, and it has given the International

---

[38] Maximo Langer, 'Universal Jurisdiction is Not Disappearing,' [2015] 13 J. of Int'l Crim. J., 245, 246
[39] *Ibid.,* 252

Criminal Court jurisdiction only over war crimes, genocide, crimes of aggression, and crimes against humanity. I fear that political pressure can often come into play when trying to get the UN, or its security council, to approve an ad hoc tribunal, or trying to get the ICC to prosecute atrocity crimes. Thus, for example, we find it unlikely that the UN will create an ad hoc tribunal to prosecute crimes of violence against women (outside of mass atrocities) or the subcategory of gender violence of pornography or that the ICC will prosecute these as crimes against humanity which we argue they are. The UN exercises its jurisdiction in a limited way such as by creating the International Criminal Court (limited to those crimes listed above), and the ad hoc tribunals such as Nuremberg, ICTY, and ICTR which dealt with atrocity crimes in specific nations/areas of the world.[40]

One major case brought under extraterritorial jurisdiction and the U.S. Alien Tort Claims Act was the civil lawsuit *Kadic v. Karadzic* (1995).[41] This involved genocidal rape, massive human rights violations that mainly targeted women, namely the ethnic

---

[40]*Ibid.*
[41]*Kadic v. Karadzic*, 70 F.3d 232 (2d Cir. 1995)

cleansing of non-Serbs through mass "rapes, torture, killings, and mutilation of women and girls" by Serbs in Croatia.[42] The defendant head of the Bosnia Serbs, Radovan Karadzic, was served when he came to the UN in New York for peace talks.[43] In 2000, a jury in New York awarded 745 million dollars in compensatory and punitive damages and granted an injunction; the U.S. Supreme Court, in refusing to review the case, let this judgment stand.[44] In my opinion, as expressed 30 years ago in *Sourcebook*, and reiterated now, civil lawsuits against pornographers for harms done to those they sexually abused in pornography and to other women who were abused as a result of their abusers imitating pornography against them is a major route victims and their advocates must take to shut down the international pornography organized crime industry which is motivated by profit. Civil remedies, which can be pursued under many theories in all nations, are not a part of this article.

---

[42]Natalie Nenadic, 'Genocide and Sexual Atrocities: Hannah Arendt's Eichmann in Jerusalem and Karadzic in New York,' [2011] 39(2) Philosophical Topics 117, 130
[43]*Ibid.*, 138
[44]*Ibid.*, 139

Universal jurisdiction enables any nation to prosecute individuals for violations of those core atrocity crimes, and/or torture, which occurred anywhere in the world, as long as national law allows for such extraterritorial jurisdiction; states, however, often limit such jurisdiction to situations where the defendant is present in the state, Langer notes.[45] Thus, using this global enforcer strategy, Israel prosecuted Eichmann, Spain prosecuted Pinochet, and Belgium prosecuted Sharon and others.[46] Cases against Nazis in Canada, the U.S., and Australia during the 1980's and 1990's were also enabled by these "no safe haven" universal concepts.[47] Belgium was pressured, by powerful nations such as the U.S. and Israel, to change its laws to disallow universal jurisdiction after it instituted universal jurisdiction prosecutions in its courts against leaders of the U.S., Iran, Chad, the Democratic Republic of Congo, Iraq, Israel, the Palestinian Authority, Cote d'Ivoire, and other nations.[48]

---

[45]*Ibid.*, 251
[46]*Ibid.*
[47]*Ibid.*
[48]Danielle Ireland-Piper, 'Prosecutions of Extraterritorial Criminal Conduct and the Abuse of Rights Doctrine,' [2013] 9(4) Utrecht L. Rev. 68, 77

The torture convention (Convention Against Torture and Other Cruel, or Inhuman Treatment) contains a provision enabling universal jurisdiction to apply to prosecutions under it.[49] We are arguing, throughout this article, that much pornography of the type we propose to outlaw and criminalize consists of images of real women, children, and men being tortured.

Coco [2018] writes about the International Law Commission work on draft articles involving crimes against humanity such as under Draft Article 7's duty to establish national jurisdiction over such crimes as well as the duty to investigate them (whenever an offender is in a state's territory).[50] He opines:

> Reminding states of their duty to establish jurisdiction over crimes against humanity may push them into a so-called 'virtuous cycle', generating an improvement in prevention and punishment of other crimes covered by international conventions, like

---

[49] *Ibid.*
[50] Antonio Coco, 'The Universal Duty to Establish Jurisdiction over, and Investigate, Crimes Against Humanity: Preliminary Remarks on Draft Articles 7, 8, 9 and 11 by the International Law Commission,' [2018] 16 J. of Int'l Crim. J. 751

terrorism, human trafficking, organized crime and corruption.⁵¹

Lastly, we must not forget that, as Ireland-Piper describes, a state can violate the "abuse of rights" doctrine if it uses its rights to impede another state from enjoying its own rights, or by using its universal rights against an individual person in a way "inconsistent with the rule of law."⁵²

B. Jus Cogens

The concept of Jus Cogens was established by the Vienna Convention on the Law of Treaties in 1969. It states in Art. 53 that a treaty that conflicts with a "peremptory norm of general international law" is void (unless or until modified by a subsequent norm) and defines a peremptory norm as one "accepted and recognized by the international

---

⁵¹Coco, 753, citing authors who are promoting a new international treaty on crimes against humanity, L.N. Sadat, 'Codifying the "Laws of Humanity" and the "Dictates of the Public Conscience": Towards a New Global Treaty on Crimes Against Humanity', in M. Bergsmo and SONG, T. (eds), *On the Proposed Crimes Against Humanity Convention* (Torkel Opsahl Academic EPublisher, 2014) 17, at 45-46
⁵²Ireland-Piper, 84

community of States as a whole as a norm from which no derogation is permitted."[53]

Thomas Weatherall explains that *jus cogens* norms transcend the interests of individual States and that individuals benefit from such norms. The animating principle of *jus cogens* is "human dignity" according to Weatherall.[54] When considering law reforms to regulate pornography, we need to "imagine reform that animates inherent dignity and worth concepts that are non-positional, but universal and unalienable," Donohue suggests.[55]

Weatherall states that *jus cogens* norms include slavery, piracy, war crimes, crimes against humanity, aggression, genocide, torture, apartheid and terrorism.[56] I believe pornography constitutes a human rights violation and a crime against humanity and involves torture or other cruel, inhuman, or degrading treatment, thus falling within international *jus cogens* norms. In addition,

---

[53] UN site, 344.
[54] Thomas Weatherall, Jus Cogens International Law and Social Contract. (2015, 2017) Cambridge University Press, 21, 32, 34
[55] Donohue, 306
[56] *Ibid.*, 212

many women and children in pornography are slaves of the human trafficking industry. Akdeniz, citing *R v. Sharpe,* described child pornography as images which "'degrade and dehumanize children.'"[57]

Saul's list of topics to which the Inter-American Court for Human Rights has applied jus cogens norm status includes prohibition of torture, cruel, inhuman or degrading treatment, discrimination, and equal protection.[58] We argue throughout this article that pornography involves each of these wrongful acts. Pornography would be considered discriminatory because it primarily preaches subordination of and discrimination against women.

In their 2013 book, Farhad Malekian and Kerstin Nordlof argued that nations are required to prohibit sexual exploitation of

---

[57] Yaman Akdeniz, *Internet Child Pornography and the Law National and International Responses* [2008, 2009] Farnham, Surrey: Ashgate Publishing, Ltd., 4 fn. 1, citing *R v Sharpe,* 2001 SCC2. File No. 27376, 26 January 2001

[58] Matthew Saul, 'Identifying Jus Cogens Norms: The Interaction of Scholars and International Judges' (May 2014) Asian Journal of International Law, 1, 13

children [we would add all persons] as an obligation *erga omnes*. They state:

> The rules of customary international criminal law have without doubt encouraged the prohibition of trafficking in persons and therefore create obligations on states to accept international legal standards regarding the prohibition of sex trafficking and the sexual exploitation of children, men and women.[59]

We admit that some might claim that prohibiting discrimination (which we claim pornography does) is not as serious a matter as genocide or atrocity crimes and does not rise to the level of an international norm.

C. Customary International Law

Ireland-Piper explains that jurisdiction based on customary international law has three bases: "nationality, territoriality, and universality."[60] The territoriality principle involves conduct that occurs within a nation's

---

[59] Farhad Malekian and Kerstin Nordlof, *Prohibition of Sexual Exploitation of Children Constituting Obligation Erga* Omnes. [2013] Newcastle upon Tyne: Cambridge Scholars Publishing, 10

[60] Ireland-Piper, 68

borders; the nationality principle enables a state to assert jurisdiction over its own national even if the wrongful conduct took place elsewhere, and; (as detailed above), the universality principle allows a state to assert jurisdiction over serious international crimes.[61] In addition, if a state believes acts are against its national interest or threaten its security, even if not illegal in another state and occurring in the other state, it can exercise extraterritorial jurisdiction under the protective principle, Ireland-Piper states.[62] Such situations might include treason, counterfeiting currency, forging official documents, economic crimes, and more.[63] We argue that violence against persons is epidemic and of such major concern and that pornography is one major tool which incites such violence.

CEDAW General Recommendation No. 35, updating No. 19, provides that the "prohibition

---

[61] *Ibid.*, 73-76
[62] *Ibid.*, 77
[63] *Ibid.*

of gender-based violence has become a norm of international customary law."[64]

Thirlway (2015) described the work of the International Law Commission on the topic of international custom as a source of law. He states that "a norm protecting human rights could thus be customary law, or contained in a treaty or result from general principles of law."[65] He points out that some scholars believe that the soft law of at least some opinions of human rights treaty bodies and committees may become "quasi-treaty obligations or some specialized form of custom."[66] In turn, he posits, if human rights law norms are considered to be rules of customary law, then they are "obligations *erga omnes*, as 'obligations . . . toward the international community as a whole.'"[67]

1. Qualified Territoriality

---

[64]Sheila Dauer, 'Human Rights Responses to Violence Against Women,' [2019] in N. Reilly (ed), *International Human Rights of Women*, Springer, Singapore, 2019, 5

[65]Hugh Thirlway, 'International Law and Practice: Human Rights in Customary Law: An Attempt to Define Some Issues,' [2015] 28 Leiden J. of Int'l Law 495, 496

[66]*Ibid.*, 501-502

[67]*Ibid.*, 499, citing the ICJ case of *Barcelona Traction*, Judgment of 5 February 1970 [1970] ICJ Rep. 32, at 33

Maillart (2019) emphasizes that, when cybercrime is involved, authorities often cannot pinpoint where a cybercrime occurred.[68] This is an important aspect which inhibits trying to combat child pornography and adult pornography on the Internet. He states that under the qualified territoriality principle, "a state can exercise jurisdiction over a crime" if either the criminal conduct or the result of the conduct took place in the state's territory.[69] In the case of cyber pornography, the conduct takes place in a state's territory when it is available on the Internet in a state.

D. Due Diligence

According to Sosa, the due diligence principle arose out of the need, internationally, to be able to assign responsibility to states for the acts of private individuals.[70]

When, as we would argue, in the case of pornography, human rights are involved, states

---

[68] Jean-Baptiste Maillart, 'The Limits of Subjective Territorial Jurisdiction in the Context of Cybercrime,' [2019] 19 ERA Forum 375

[69] *Ibid.*, 377

[70] Lorena Sosa, *Intersectionality In the Human Rights Legal Framework On Violence Against Women: At the Centre Or The Margins?* [2017] Cambridge, UK, Cambridge University Press, 53

have certain obligations under international law. Bjarnadottir describes these as "the obligation to respect, to protect, and to fulfil human rights."[71]

A report was issued by Yakin Erturk, the second UN Special Rapporteur on Violence Against Women, to provide guidance on applying due diligence to violence against women. Under it, due diligence requires states to conduct effective investigations of crimes and prosecute and sanction violent acts by private actors and the state, to provide effective judicial remedies, provide victims with access to justice and respectful treatment, ensure reparations, identify women more at risk, and modify cultural and social practices which are stereotyped or based on superiority or inferiority.[72]

---

[71] Maria Run Bjarnadottir, 'Does the Internet Limit Human Rights Protection? The Case of Revenge Porn,' [2016] 7(3) J. of Intellectual Property, Information Technology and E-Commerce Law 204-215, 204

[72] *Ibid.*, 17-18, fn. 120, Special Rapporteur on Violence Against Women, its Causes and Consequences, 'Integration of the Human Rights of Women and the Gender Perspective: Violence Against Women: The Due Diligence Standard as a Tool for the Elimination of Violence Against Women,' [20 January 2006] E/CN.4/2006/61

Due diligence was described in CEDAW Gen. Recommendation 35 as underpinning the CEDAW convention, and making parties responsible for human rights violations if they "fail to take all appropriate measures to prevent as well as to investigate, prosecute, punish and provide reparation for acts or omissions by non-State actors which result in gender-based violence against women" and that it includes "actions by corporations operating extraterritorially."[73] Randall and Venkatesh described the international due diligence obligation as one in which "states are obliged to prevent, investigate, punish, and provide remedies for violations of human rights, regardless of whether the acts are committee by state or nonstate actors."[74]

The CEDAW Committee adopted the due diligence typology of state obligations to respect, protect, promote and fulfil the right of

---

[73] CEDAW Committee, General Recommendation No. 35 on Gender-based Violence Against Women, Updating General Recommendation No. 19, 14 July 2017, CEDAW/C/GC/35, Par. 20(b), 8

[74] Melanie Randall and Vasanthi Venkatesh, 'Symposium On The International Legal Obligation To Criminalize Marital Rape Criminalizing Sexual Violence Against Women In Intimate Relationships: State Obligations Under Human Rights Law,' [2016] 109 AJIL Unbound 189, 190

women to not be subjected to gender-based violence.[75] Chinkin explains that respect means the government must provide the means and structures to effectively combat such violence, and to make certain that all its criminal, civil, administrative and labor laws do not discriminate against women.[76] She explains that the duty to protect and guarantee involves taking positive actions to prevent violence against women both by state and private actors, and that lastly, the duty to fulfil means taking long-term actions for enjoying human rights.[77]

The Inter-American Court of Human Rights has identified the positive obligations of states as "prevention, investigation, punishment and redress of human rights violations, and the obligation to prevent impunity."[78] Stedman reports that the IACHR stated that there is an

---

[75] CEDAW Committee, Gen. Recomm. No. 28, n2, par. 9
[76] Christine Chinkin, 'Addressing Violence Against Women in the Commonwealth Within States' Obligations Under International Law,' [2014] 40(3) Commonwealth L. Bull. 471, 478
[77] *Ibid.*, 279
[78] Brooke Stedman, 'The Leap from Theory to Practice: Snapshot of Women's Rights Through A Legal Lens,' [2013] 29(77) Merkourios 4, 8, citing Velasquez Rodriguez v. Honduras (Judgment) Inter-American Court of Human Rights Ser. C No. 4 (1988)

international consensus that "'a State's failure to act with due diligence to protect women from violence constitutes a form of discrimination, and denies women their right to equality before the law.'"[79] We believe that this interpretation of due diligence should be applied to the obligation of states to protect women from violent hardcore, extreme, and nonconsensual pornography.

Chapter Four: To What Extent Do Existing International Treaties and Agencies Regulate Pornography?

While child pornography is heavily regulated internationally, regionally, and nationally, we have found no evidence of adult pornography being *directly* regulated at the international level or in international law other than the early treaties against obscenity mentioned herein. We will argue, below, that certain existing international treaties as well as concepts of jus cogens, or, as an alternative, customary international law make it conceivable that IBSA and extreme and violent as well as nonconsensual adult pornography could be combatted under existing laws. Some

---

[79]*Ibid.*, 10, quoting Lenahan (Gonzales) v United States (Merits) Inter-American Commission on Human Rights Report (Case 12.626) No 80/1 (21 July 2011)

states regulate adult pornography under concepts of morality and health, obscenity or indecency concepts, or extremity or the nonconsensual nature of the image based sexual abuse contents. We do not examine national laws in this paper.

A. ICCPR

The International Covenant on Civil and Political Rights (1966)[80] Art. 2 sets out obligations of state parties to ensure that the rights set forth in the treaty are enjoyed by all persons in their territories without discrimination, including based on sex. Parties are to undertake to ensure that men and women enjoy these rights equally under Art. 3. Art. 7 provides that "no one shall be subjected to torture or to cruel, inhuman or degrading treatment or punishment." (ICCPR and pornography as torture is addressed in detail later in this article.) Art. 8 provides that no one shall be held in slavery and that slavery shall be prohibited by the states. Art. 20 requires states to enact laws prohibiting advocacy of "national, racial or religious hatred that constitutes incitement to discrimination, hostility or violence." This needs to be amended to add sex

---

[80] Treaty as reprinted in Bisset, 34-45

as a category so that pornography, which incites violence and hatred toward women, is outlawed. We do not address, in detail, various international treaties and customs which outlaw incitement to crime. Art. 26 requires "effective protection against discrimination" including on the basis of sex and that laws prohibit discrimination. This treaty is overseen by a Human Rights Committee (Art. 28).

We would argue that states have an obligation to restrict the publication and dissemination of violent, degrading pornography under ICCPR based on General Comment 28 (non-binding soft law) of the Human Rights Committee which administers the covenant:

> As the publication and dissemination of obscene and pornographic material which portrays women and girls as objects of violence or degrading or inhuman treatment is likely to promote these kinds of treatment of women and girls, States parties should provide information about legal measures to

restrict the publication and dissemination of such material.[81]

The First Optional Protocol to the ICCPR (1966) provides for the Committee to receive and consider communications from individuals who claim they are victims of violations of any of the rights in the Covenant.[82]

Randall and Venkatesh state that under ICCPR Art. 4(2), the right to life is a nonderogable right. The posit that the CEDAW Committee, the Human Rights Committee, and the Committee Against Torture have said that violence against women, including marital rape, "can breach fundamental rights to life, liberty and security of person, to nondiscrimination and equal protection under the law, and to freedom from torture."[83] We believe that child pornography and hardcore extreme, violent, and nonconsensual pornography are forms of violence against women, of torture, and breach the rights to life, liberty and security of persons in violation of ICCPR. Therefore, the multitude of states who

---

[81] MacKinnon, 1010, citing Human Rights Comm., 68th Sess., 1834th Mtg., *General Comment No. 28* par. 22, U.N. Doc. CCPR/C/21/Rev.1/Add. 10 (2000)
[82] Bisset, 45
[83] Randall and Venkatesh, 191

ratified ICCPR have an obligation to ban such pornography from their cyberspace, to take all possible measures to remove it from cyberspace, to investigate, prosecute, and punish those responsible for producing, disseminating, and possessing such pornography, and to provide victims with reparations in criminal and civil remedies of national laws.

B. Pornography as a Form of Trafficking In Persons Under International Laws Against Human Trafficking

It can be argued that pornography falls under international law because it is sexual exploitation, sex trafficking, and prostitution. Catharine A. MacKinnon wrote in 2005 that "pornography is one way women and children are trafficked for sex" and we agree. Real people are rented out to make pornography and the materials are then "sold for a buyer's sexual use." This, she argues, involves commercial sexual exploitation and makes prostitutes out of women who appear in the images.[84]

---

[84] Catharine A. MacKinnon, 'Pornography as Trafficking,' [2005] 26(4) Mich. J. of Int'l Law 993

MacKinnon explains how international law includes pornography, relying on the 2000 Palermo Protocol's[85] definition of trafficking in persons. The Palermo Protocol obligates state signatories to "criminalize and take action to prevent all forms of human trafficking" including sexual exploitation.[86] The definition of trafficking in persons under this protocol includes trafficking, prostitution of persons, and other forms of sexual exploitation which makes pornography sex trafficking, MacKinnon states:

> For pornography, women and children are recruited, transported, provided, and obtained for sex acts on account of which, typically, money is given to pornography pimps and received by lesser pimps. Then, each time the pornography is commercially exchanged, the trafficking continues as the women and children in it are transported and provided for sex,

---

[85](Palermo Protocol), Protocol to Prevent, Suppress and Punish Trafficking in Persons, Especially Women and Children, supplementing the U.N. Convention Against Transnational Organized Crime, G.A. Res. 55/25, U.N. GAOR, 55th Sess. Annex II, U.N. Doc. A/55/383 (2000).

[86]Rabia Akhtar, 'The Neglected Boys of War: Trapped In A Vicious Cycle of Slavery and Sexual Abuse,' [2019] 3 J. of Traff. And Human Exploitation 179, 186-187

sold, and bought again. Doing all these things for the purpose of exploiting the prostitution of others-which pornography intrinsically does-makes it trafficking in persons.[87]

Regarding children, MacKinnon notes that Art. 3 of the Convention Concerning the Prohibition and Immediate Action for the Elimination of the Worst Forms of Child Labor (1999) prohibits using, procuring or offering a child for prostitution "for the production of pornography or pornographic performances," as well as slavery including the "sale and trafficking of children . . . ."[88] MacKinnon sees an international consensus evolving around laws against commercial sexual exploitation (which she defines as including pornography and the "global sex industry").[89] She also describes most pornography as being made by "slaves" who lack other choices in life and that pornography results from crimes against women and children.[90] This reality, of course, also brings the issue of pornography and its victims who are forced to participate in its

---

[87] *Ibid.*, 1003-1004
[88] *Ibid.*, 1004
[89] *Ibid.*, 994
[90] *Ibid.*, 995, 1001

production, under international laws against slavery in my view.

Among the preparatory remarks of the United Nations Educational, Scientific, and Cultural Organization (UNESCO) regarding the 1949 Convention for the Suppression of the Traffic in Persons and of the Exploitation of Prostitution of Others, was a proposal to restrict circulation or display of obscene works through television, radio, or cinema as a measure for preventing prostitution.[91]

We believe that child pornography and hardcore extreme, violent, and nonconsensual pornography are forms of sexual exploitation because real persons were sexually abused and trafficked in to produce it. Therefore, states who ratified conventions against human trafficking (including sexual exploitation) have an obligation to ban such pornography from their cyberspace, to take all possible measures to remove it from cyberspace, to investigate, prosecute, and punish those responsible for producing, disseminating, and possessing such pornography, and to provide victims with

---

[91] *Ibid.*, 1002-1003, citing U.N. Econ. & Soc. Council [ECOSOC], at 4, U.N. Doc. E/CN.5/115/Add.5 (1949) (commenting on Art. 17)

reparations in criminal and civil remedies of national laws.

C. Child Pornography Regulations in International Law

Child pornography on the internet is covered in three international instruments: The UNCRC, the CRC Optional Protocol on the Sale of Children, Child Prostitution and Child Pornography and the U.N. Protocol to Prevent, Suppress, and Punish Trafficking in Persons.[92] It is important to emphasize that the Optional Protocol enables child sexual offenses to be enforced extra-territorially.[93] It requires State Parties to have domestic criminal laws (with "appropriate penalties") which prohibit, under Art. 3.1.(c) "producing, distributing, disseminating, importing, exporting, offering, selling or possessing . . . child pornography as defined in Art. 2."[94] Other laws against child pornography can be found at the regional and national levels. For example, the 22 December

---

[92] Alexander Kalim, 'Addressing The Gap in International Instruments Governing Internet Child Pornography,' [2013] 21 Common Law Conspectus, 428, 437

[93] Kalim, 439

[94] Alison Bisset, ed., [2018] *Blackstone's International Human Rights Documents 11th Edition,* Oxford University Press, 112-113, reprint of the law

2003 Framework Decision of the EU Council on combatting the sexual exploitation of children and child pornography requires all members states of the EU to "criminalize the production, distribution, dissemination or transmission of child pornography" and the supplying, making available, acquiring or possessing child pornography.[95] We must recognize that child pornography is sexual abuse and sexual exploitation.

The Council of the European Union, in 1997, created common rules to fight the sexual exploitation of children, and, in a Framework Decision on such exploitation and child pornography in 2004, created common provisions on criminalization and sanctions, assisting victims, and jurisdiction.[96] Online child pornography and making child pornography a criminal offense with minimum sanctions in the EU were addressed in a 2011

---

[95] Akdeniz, 13

[96] Amanda Haasz, 'Underneath it All: Policing International Child Pornography on the Dark Web,' [2016] 43(2) Syracuse J. Int'l L. & Com. 353, 364, citing Council Joint Action 97/154/JHA, 1997 O.J. (L63) 7, 7 (EU) and the 2004 Framework Decision 2004/68/JHA, 2004 O.J. (L13) 44 (EU)

Directive.[97] The Council of Europe's European Convention on Human Rights, enforced by the European Court of Human Rights enables causes of action under Art. 3 for failure to protect against child abuse, including a state's failure to "take adequate measures to prevent further abuse" or failure to provide preventive measures such as criminal sanctions.[98] A 2011 report explains the state obligations and lists ECtHR cases on the topics of child sexual abuse and child pornography.[99]

We believe that the multitude of states who ratified CRC, or the Optional Protocol to the CRC, and/or other treaties which prohibit sexual exploitation of children, including, for example, labor laws, and broad human rights treaties such as ICCPR, have an obligation to ban such pornography from their cyberspace, to take all possible measures to remove it from cyberspace, to investigate, prosecute, and punish those responsible for producing, disseminating, and possessing such

---

[97]Haasz, 364, citing Council Directive 2011/92/EU, 2011 O.J. (L. 335)
[98]European Court of Human Rights, 'Research Report: Child Sexual Abuse and Child Pornography in the Court's Case-Law,' [2011], 5
[99]*Ibid.*

pornography, and to provide victims with reparations in criminal or civil remedies of national laws.

D. CEDAW, Violence Against Women, and Fighting Pornography

Meghan Campbell explains that the Committee which interprets the Convention on the Elimination of all Forms of Discrimination Against Women (CEDAW) is working with the Optional Protocol to the treaty which was passed by the UN General Assembly in Resolution 54/4 in October 1999. The OP-CEDAW allows the Committee to consider communications from individuals who claim a state party to the treaty has breached it.[100] However, the decisions of the Committee are not binding on the nations, unfortunately.[101]

The original CEDAW treaty does not prohibit violence against women but the CEDAW Committee Chair from 2007 to 2008 explains that it has been incorporated into the treaty considered as a form of discrimination

---

[100] Meghan Campbell, 'Women's Rights and the Convention on the Elimination of all Forms of Discrimination Against Women: Unlocking the Potential of the Optional Protocol,' [2016] Nordic Journal of Human Rights, 34:4, 247, 248
[101] *Ibid.,* 251

against women.[102] General Recommendation Nos. 12 and 19 to CEDAW explain that propagating pornography and other commercial exploitation of women as sex objects instead of as individuals contributes to gender-based violence.[103] Although Committee recommendations are not legally binding, they are significant because they regard gender-based violence as an international human rights law issue and acknowledge the correlation between pornography and violence against women.[104]

a. <u>States Authorize IPV and Image-Based Sexual Abuse</u>

Rose argues that states promote and condone the systematic subordination of women even if state actors do not, themselves, commit the acts of intimate partner violence.[105]

---

[102] Dubravka Simonovic, 'Global and Regional Standards on Violence Against Women: The Evolution and Synergy of the CEDAW and Istanbul Conventions,' [2014] 36(3) Human Rights Quarterly 590, 599
[103] Frida Nilsson, 'The Balance Between Patriarchal Oppression and Sexual Freedom: A Human Rights Based Approach to Pornography,' [2009] Paper presented in Human Rights Studies at Lunds Universitet; Giunta, 1997, 58
[104] Giunta, 58
[105] Rose, 33

Among the ways in which states authorize such violence, Rose states is by endorsing the sex industry which correlates with the "prevalence of sexual and domestic violence" and subjugation of women.[106] Halverson states that gender-based torture fills the pornography industry and that such companies are intentionally and systematically causing severe physical and mental suffering to real women "in order to profit and to degrade the female gender."[107] Giunta describes pornography as a type of hate speech propaganda inciting violence against women. Pornography promotes violence against women by depicting them as "deserving and enjoying degrading treatment" and begging for "pain and humiliation."[108]

Article I of CEDAW[109] defines discrimination against women as: . . . any distinction, exclusion or restriction made on the basis of sex which has the effect or purpose of impairing or nullifying the recognition,

---

[106] Rose, 36
[107] Halverson, 1
[108] Giunta, 52
[109] References to CEDAW are taken from Bisset, and from https://www.ohchr.org/EN/HRBodies/CEDAW/Pages/Introduction.aspx

enjoyment or exercise by women, irrespective of their marital status, on the basis of equality of men and women, of human rights and fundamental freedoms in their political, economic, social, cultural, civil or any other field.

Article 2 of CEDAW imposes obligations on state parties. It requires them to take affirmative actions to eliminate discrimination against women. This is to be done by passing laws prohibiting such discrimination and imposing sanctions. The obligation includes a requirement to make certain that organizations and persons do not discriminate against women, to repeal all laws which discriminate against women, and to ensure that "competent national tribunals" and other public institutions protect women against discrimination.

Article 6 obligates states to "take all appropriate measures, including legislation, to suppress all forms of traffic in women and exploitation of prostitution of women.

Optional Protocol Art. 2 enables private individuals or groups, under a state's jurisdiction, to submit communications to the

CEDAW Committee alleging to be victims of the violation of any rights in CEDAW by the state party. Here again it must be emphasized that these complaints are against states, not private individuals or organizations.

CEDAW General Recommendation No. 19 (1992) "explicitly defines violence against women as a problem of inequality." Discrimination includes "violence 'directed against a woman because she is a woman or that affects women disproportionately.'" Gender-based violence is defined as a form of sex discrimination. Violence against women is considered a human rights violation. Under Rec. No. 19, States are responsible for acts of private persons (for example, a domestic abuser) "when they fail to act with due diligence to prevent violations or to investigate and punish acts of violence." Unfortunately, CEDAW lacks an enforcement mechanism.

CEDAW General Recommendation No. 28, par. 9 (2010) addressed the core obligations of states under Art. 2 stating that they are to "respect, protect and fulfil women's rights to non-discrimination and the enjoyment of de jure and de facto equality."

CEDAW General Recommendation No. 35 par. 16 (2017) states that gender-based violence against women "may amount to torture or cruel, inhuman or degrading treatment in certain circumstances, including in cases of rape, domestic violence or harmful practices, among others" and may sometimes be international crimes.

We believe that hardcore extreme, violent, and nonconsensual pornography are forms of violence against women and of discrimination against women in that pornography disproportionately affects women and, therefore, violates CEDAW and its Optional Protocol. Therefore, the states who ratified those treaties have an obligation to ban such pornography from their cyberspace, to take all possible measures to remove it from cyberspace, to investigate, prosecute, and punish those responsible for producing, disseminating, and possessing such pornography, and to provide victims with reparations in criminal and civil remedies of national laws.

E. The Rome Statute of the International Criminal Court and Crimes Against Humanity

If Image-Based Sexual Abuse, child pornography, nonconsensual pornography and extreme or violent pornography were to be considered a crime against humanity under international law, it would give the International Criminal Court the jurisdiction to prosecute both governments (only those which are member states of ICC) who promote or condone such abuse or fail to protect victims or prevent such abuse, as well as organizations (here international or national organized crime enterprises) who produce and promote such pornography. It would also give each nation, under concepts of universality and extraterritorial jurisdiction (if such concepts are part of the nation's law and if the offender or offenders are present in the nation) the right to arrest and try them for such crimes against humanity which it is their obligation under international law to do.

Meeting the Criteria for Crimes Against Humanity:

Art. 5 (1) of the Rome Statute of the ICC state that "the jurisdiction of the court shall be limited to the most serious crimes of concern to the international community as a whole."[110] We would argue that child pornography and Image-Based Sexual Abuse are such serious crimes in that they are crimes against humanity.

Crimes Against Humanity are defined in Article 7 of the Rome Statute (in relevant parts):[111]

1. For the purpose of this Statute, "crime against humanity" means any of the following acts when committed as part of a widespread or systematic attack directed against any civilian population, with knowledge of the attack:

> (c) Enslavement [including trafficking in persons under 2. (c)]
> (e) Imprisonment or other severe deprivation of physical liberty in violation of fundamental rules of international law;
> (f) Torture;
> (g) Rape, sexual slavery, enforced prostitution, forced pregnancy, enforced sterilization, or any other form of sexual

---

[110] Rome Statute of the ICC, Accessed Internet 29 June 2019 at http://legal.un.org/icc/statute/99_corr/cstatute.htm
[111] *Ibid.*

violence of comparable gravity [which we argue pornography is];

(h) Persecution against any identifiable group or collectivity on [categories omitted]. . . . gender [male and female] or other grounds that are universally recognized as impermissible under international law, in connection with any act referred to in this paragraph or any crime within the jurisdiction of the Court;

(k) Other inhumane acts of a similar character intentionally causing great suffering, or serious injury to body or to mental or physical health. [We argue that this could include pornography making and dissemination.]

Attacks directed against any civilian population involve a course of conduct of multiple acts in Par. 1 "pursuant to or in furtherance of a State or organizational policy to commit such attack" [2(a)]. We believe it can be demonstrated that pornography (offenses) are done to further State polices and organizational (organized criminal) (or other organizations such as websites which promote pornography) policies, in some nations.

The ICC has held that non-state actors "are possible perpetrators of crimes against humanity."[112] However, to convict someone, it must be shown that he or she had knowledge that his actions were part of a widespread or systematic attack on a civilian population.[113] That criteria might be difficult to meet, which suggests this ICC criteria should be amended.

Trafficking in persons is considered sexual slavery, Joseph states.[114]

For the purpose of paragraph 1:

> (e) "Torture" means the intentional infliction of severe pain or suffering, whether physical or mental, upon a person in the custody or under the control of the accused; except that torture shall not include pain or suffering arising only from, inherent in or incidental to, lawful sanctions;

---

[112] Joshua H. Joseph, 'Gender and International Law: How the International Criminal Court Can Bring Justice to Victims of Sexual Violence,' [2008] 18 Tex. J. Women & L. 61, 72, citing Prosecutor v. Tadic, Case No. IT-94-1-T, Opinion and Judgment pp 654-55 (7 May 1997).

[113] *Ibid.*, 73
[114] *Ibid.*, 85

(g) "Persecution" means the intentional and severe deprivation of fundamental rights contrary to international law by reason of the identity of the group or collectivity;

1. <u>Image-Based Sexual Abuse Production Involves Crimes which are actionable under the Rome Statute Crimes Against Humanity provisions.</u>

Among the crimes against humanity which we believe may be committed in individual situations of IBSA are: rape, murder, enslavement, imprisonment or deprivation of physical liberty, torture, "Rape, sexual slavery, enforced prostitution . . . or any other form of sexual violence of comparable gravity," persecution against women, and "Other inhumane acts of a similar character intentionally causing great suffering, or serious injury to body or to mental or physical health." We argue that filming as well as publicizing images of a person's sexual abuse is, in itself, a form of sexual violence of gravity and an inhumane act with causes great suffering and serious injury to mental/emotional health.

2. <u>IPV and Image-Based Sexual Abuse Are Serious Crimes Which Impact</u>

Many Persons Across the World

IBSA involves acts (under the Rome Statute) committed as part of a widespread or systematic attack directed against any civilian population (here, women) with knowledge of the attack as required by the statute.

It also involves "a course of conduct involving the multiple commission of acts referred to in paragraph 1 against any civilian population, pursuant to or in furtherance of a State or organizational policy to commit such attack"

b. Organizational policies are involved in these acts committed by organized criminal and racketeering enterprises).

F. <u>Convention Against Torture (See Chapter Below)</u>

G. African Union Regional Treaty

The Protocol to the African Charter on Human and Peoples' Rights on the Rights of Women in Africa (in force 2005) requires state parties to "take legislative and administrative measures to prevent the exploitation and abuse of women in advertising and pornography."[115]

H. The Istanbul Convention

A newer convention of the Council of Europe, the Istanbul Convention on Preventing and Combating Violence Against Women and Domestic Violence (2011), ratified by 22 states as of 2017, requires states, under due diligence, to intervene and punish crimes against women, even if committed by private parties, and to adopt measures to prevent such crimes and protect victims of abuse.[116] Art. 3(a) of the Istanbul Convention defines violence against women as "all acts of gender-based violence that result in, or are likely to result in, physical, sexual, psychological or economic harm or suffering to women, including threats of such acts, coercion or arbitrary deprivation of liberty, whether occurring in public or private

---

[115]MacKinnon, 2005, 1009, citing the Protocol to the African Charter on Human and Peoples' Rights on the Rights of Women in Africa, art. 13(m), 11 July 2003, O.A.U. Doc. CAB/LEG/66.6 (entered into force 26 November 2005)

[116]Sara De Vido, 'The Ratification of the Council of Europe Istanbul Convention by the EU: A Step Forward in the Protection of Women from Violence in the European Legal System,' [2017] 9(2) Eur. J. of Legal Studies 69, 71-73

life."[117] Violent and extreme and nonconsensual pornography would certainly be covered by aspects of this convention because, for those who are filmed in it, it involves physical and/or sexual harm or suffering, as well as psychological harm. Economic harm could encompass the economic losses all women suffer as a result of pornography promoting discrimination toward women. It is interesting that this convention covers domestic violence and it is well known that domestic abusers often use pornography against their victims.

I. The United Nations Human Rights Council

The UNHRC was created by Resolution 60/251 of the UN General Assembly on 15 March 2006, replacing the Commission on Human Rights. This resolution reaffirmed the principles in the UDHR, the UN Charter, the Vienna Declaration, the ICCPR, the ICESCR and "other human rights instruments" and provided for it to do universal periodic reviews of state actions on human and humanitarian

---

[117] Lisa Grans, 'The Istanbul Convention and the Positive Obligation to Prevent Violence,' [2018] 18 Human Rights L. Rev. 133, 136-137

rights.[118] The Resolution emphasized the responsibilities of all States, under the UN Charter, "to respect human rights and fundamental freedoms for all" (without any distinctions, including sex and many other categories).[119] Beneath the Council, a think-tank style Advisory Committee was established having the authority to accept individual and group complaints about "consistent patterns of gross and reliably attested violations of all human rights and all fundamental freedoms occurring in any part of the world and under any circumstances."[120] To use this procedure, domestic remedies must have been exhausted or ineffective or taking an unreasonable amount of time to resolve.[121] While this appears, again, to be a form of soft law without any way of enforcement, such a procedure could be used to bring the issue of child pornography, IBSA, and extreme, violent and nonconsensual pornography in cyberspace to the attention of UN human rights authorities and, through media coverage, the world. That, in turn, could motivate some states to take action to end such human rights abuses.

---

[118]Bissett, treaties reprinted, 244-247
[119]*Ibid.*, 244
[120]Advisory Committee, Para 85, in Bissett, 254
[121]Advisory Committee, Para 87(d), in Bissett, 255

J. Special Rapporteur 2018 and Online Violence Against Women

In 2018, the Report of the Special Rapporteur on Violence Against Women addressed the issue of online violence against women and girls as a human rights matter. It seems strange that this report states that "online pornography and virtual manifestations of violence in video games, or violent interactive environments" are outside the scope of the report.[122] We would differ and argue that the major form of online violence against women is pornography and that it should have been addressed at length in a report about online violence toward women. The report did opine that human rights which are protected offline should also be protected online (Par. 17) It also claimed that risk of harm results from online pornography (Par. 27) and called the "non-consensual distribution of intimate contents" a form of violence against women (Par. 33) and a violation of rights to privacy (Par. 57). The report wrongly identified

---

[122]Report of the Special Rapporteur on Violence Against Women, Its Causes and Consequences On Online Violence Against Women and Girls from a Human Rights Perspective, [18 June 2018], A/HRC/38/47, 7

online anonymity as an important way for women to use to avoid discrimination and stigma (instead of reporting the role such anonymity plays in flooding the internet with pornography) (Par. 60).

Importantly, this report cited CEDAW, Art. 2(e) as giving states a "human rights obligation" to require state agents (under direct responsibility) and non-state agents (under due diligence) to refrain from acts of discrimination or violence against women (Par. 62). The due diligence obligations are to "prevent, investigate and punish acts of violence against women committed by private companies, such as Internet intermediaries . . . ."[123] What is bizarre about this statement is that the majority of acts of violence in question, on the Internet, involve pornography, which the report claims not to cover. The report states that states should prohibit and criminalize "online violence against women, in particular the non-consensual distribution of intimate images, online harassment and stalking" (Par. 101).

K. Vienna Declaration and Program of Action (25 June 1993)

---

[123] *Ibid.*, paragraphs as cited

This was a non-binding declaration of the World Conference on Human Rights. Importantly, it emphasized that states have a responsibility, to conform to the Charter of the United Nations, to "encourage respect for human rights and fundamental freedoms for all and in the equal rights of men and women and of nations large and small."[124] This declaration emphasized that women and girls have universal human rights including full participation in such rights and the right to discrimination based on sex to be eliminated. It states that: "Gender-based violence and all forms of sexual harassment and exploitation, including those resulting from cultural prejudice and international trafficking, are incompatible with the dignity and worth of the human person, and must be eliminated."[125]

L. Conclusions Regarding Obligations of States

We believe that child pornography, IBSA, and hardcore extreme, violent, and nonconsensual pornography are forms of

---

[124]OHCHR, Vienna Declaration and Program of Action, 1993, 1
[125]*Ibid.*, par. 18, p. 3

violence against persons, of torture, and breach the rights to life, liberty and security of persons in violation of the IDHR, the UN Charter, ICCPR and CEDAW (regarding women). We argue that such pornography is required to be criminalized by state parties to treaties under ICCPR, CEDAW, the ICC (Rome Statute) as a crime against humanity, CAT (as torture or other cruel, inhuman or degrading treatment), the CRC and Optional Protocol thereto (concerning children) and international treaties against trafficking in persons including sexual exploitation (which pornography is). Therefore, the multitude of states who ratified any or all of these treaties have an obligation to ban such pornography from their cyberspace, to take all possible measures to remove it from cyberspace, to investigate, prosecute, and punish those responsible for producing, disseminating, and possessing such pornography, and to provide victims with reparations in criminal and civil remedies of their national laws.

Under their due diligence obligations concerning human rights law states are required to prevent as well as to investigate, prosecute, punish and provide reparation for acts or omissions by non-State actors regarding the above-mentioned pornography-related treaty provisions. It is important to remember that most human rights violations, including these, logically, have to be addressed, and hopefully resolved, at the national levels of states under principles of subsidiarity and sovereignty instead of ending up on the agendas of international or regional human rights bodies or courts.

Chapter Five: Is Or Can Torture Pornography Be Regulated By International Law?

A. Violent and Extreme Pornography and Torture

According to the National Center on Sexual Exploitation, the pornography industry which creates "hardcore" Internet pornography "intentionally causes severe physical and mental suffering to the women filmed or photographed, and it should therefore be recognized as torture" under international law.[126] We agree. The Center specifically asked the United Nations Special Rapporteur on Torture to consider pornography to be a form of torture in its expected report on gender perspectives of torture. Mickelwait (2017) states that "BDSM torture sex is physically and mentally harmful for those who are victims of this kind of aggressive and abusive sexual torture."[127] She argues that engaging in such

---

[126] Haley Halverson, 'United Nations Special Rapporteur on Torture Report: The Gender-Based Torture Found in the Pornography Industry. The National Center on Sexual Exploitation. Accessed Internet: 21 June 2019

[127] Laila Mickelwait, 'BDSM Torture Porn and the law,' [18 August 2017] The New Jurist, 1, Accessed Internet 16 July 2019

sex "can be classified as a crime and a violation of human rights."[128]

DeKeseredy and Hall-Sanchez described "gonzo" pornography as that which involves females portrayed as subordinate to men whose main role is to provide sex to men. It involves hard-core, "body-punishing sex" such as brutal gang rape, slapping, choking, painful anal penetration, violent sex, or oral, vaginal, and anal penetration at the same time.[129]

In Japan, the pornography film industry is creating torture pornography at the request of pornography consumers according to Yamamoto, Norma, and Weerasinghe who state that online forums are used to recruit men to participate in gang rapes.[130] The authors state: "Japanese torture pornography employs various methods to abuse women, including punching; kicking; penetration of the genitals, mouth and anus; gagging; forced ingestion of

---

[128] *Ibid.,* 1

[129] Walter S. DeKeserdy and Amanda Hallo-Sanchez, 'Adult Pornography and Violence Against Women in the Hearthland: Results from a Rural Southeast Ohio Study,' [2016] Violence Against Women, 1-20, 2-3

[130] Yukino Yamamoto, Caroline Norma, and Ruwan Dep Weerasinghe, 'Consumer Involvement in Japanese Pornography Productions,' [2018] 3(2) Dignity: A J. on Sexual Exploitation and Violence 1, 2

water, alcohol, and urine; water torture; suffocation using vacuum sealable plastic bags; and burning."[131]

B. Torture Pornography and the Universal Declaration and ICCPR

It is important to emphasize that the international community, through the United Nations, has recognized prohibition of torture as a norm of international law for some time. Although the Universal Declaration of Human Rights (1948) is not binding on states, it establishes the universal belief in Art. 5 that "no one shall be subjected to torture or to cruel, inhuman or degrading treatment or punishment." We argue that torture pornography and violent pornography are torture and/or cruel, inhuman or degrading treatment. Similar conduct is also prohibited by ICCPR as described above.

C. Torture Cannot be Consented To

If a person is accused of torture, it does not matter if he or she argues that the victim consented to the "torture, serious harm, abuse,

---

[131] *Ibid.*, 13

assault and battery" according to Michelwait.[132] I concur.

A major case before the ECtHR, *Laskey, Jaggard and Brown v. United Kingdom* (1997) addressed this issue.[133] We use this case as an example of how courts could tackle the underlying acts of sexual abuse found in torture pornography. Video films were found involving the defendants and up to 44 other homosexual men detailing sadomasochistic acts. The court noted that the acts were consensual "and were conducted in private for no apparent purpose other than the achievement of sexual gratification."[134] The court described the content of the videos as showing torture.

After losing before the courts of the U.K., the defendants brought the case to the ECtHR claiming that Art. 8 of the ECHR was breached as an interference in their right to privacy. However, Art. 8.2 provides that that right cannot be interfered with by a public authority "except such as is in accordance with the law and is necessary in a democratic society in

---

[132] Mickelwait, 1
[133] *Laskey, Jaggard and Brown v United Kingdom* [1997] Available at http://hudoc.echr.coe.int/eng?i=001-58021
[134] *Laskey,* I.8

the interests of national security, public safety or the economic well-being of the country, for the prevention of disorder or crime, for the protection of health or morals, or for the protection of the rights and freedoms of others."

The defendants in Laskey argued that the acts done were consensual and did not involve serious injury. The court found that the government could prohibit acts of violence such as genital torture because of possible danger of physical injury or harm and despite a victim's consent. (paras. 40-41) Using the Margin of Appreciation doctrine which leaves decisions on some issues up to national authorities, the court found that states can regulate activities that cause physical harm which was demonstrated in this case. (para. 45) It concluded that the law was necessary for the protection of health (and proportionate to address the problem). (paras. 49-50) I agree with this court decision because the case clearly involved acts which could cause physical harm to the persons featured in the pornography, making consent irrelevant and enabling the state to regulate such acts to protect health and morals.

D. Torture Pornography and the Convention Against Torture

Although not all nations have signed and ratified the Convention Against Torture and Other Cruel, Inhuman or Degrading Treatment or Punishment (1984), its existence can be used to support the argument, made by Weatherall, above, that prohibition of torture is *jus cogens*, a norm of general international law. Under CAT, Articles 2 and 16, State parties to the treaty are obligated to take national measures to prevent torture and "other acts of cruel, inhuman or degrading treatment or punishment" in their jurisdictions according to the 2002 Optional Protocol to the treaty.[135]

Juan E. Mendez, the U.N. Special Rapporteur on Torture, wrote about how international law can eradicate torture, claiming that "torture and other cruel, inhuman, or degrading treatment . . . is absolutely prohibited by international law."[136] Of the 195 United Nations member states, 158

---

[135] Bisset, 84

[136] Juan E. Mendez, 'How International Law Can Eradicate Torture: A Response To Cynics,' [2016] 22 Southwestern J. of Int'l L. 247

have ratified the UN Convention Against Torture, he states. In a similar way to slavery and genocide, the absolute prohibition on torture and other ill treatment [including cruel, inhuman or degrading treatment or punishment] has the status, under international law, as "a *jus cogens* or peremptory, non-derogable norm," according to Mendez.[137] He describes such norms as:

> Norms that embrace customary international laws that are so universal and derived from values so fundamental to the international community that they are considered binding on all nations irrespective of a state's consent.[138]

Because these norms relating to torture are peremptory, states can exercise universal jurisdiction to prosecute torturers even if the crime took place outside the nation's territory and even if the perpetrators and the victims are citizens of other states, Mendez claims, citing CAT arts. 4 and 6.[139]

---

[137] *Ibid.*, 249-250, 255
[138] Mendez, 250, citing the Vienna Convention on the Law of Treaties, arts. 53, 64, May 23, 1969, 1155 U.N.T.S. 331
[139] *Ibid.*, 250-251.

Under CAT, arts. 4, 7, and 12, each act of torture gives rise to the need to investigate, prosecute, and punish the wrongdoer, Mendez claims.[140] In such cases, intent to commit an act, or an omission that inflicts severe pain and suffering, for example, rape, is sufficient, he states. Negligence can qualify as as cruel, inhuman or degrading treatment, he adds.[141]

When there is an armed conflict, involvement of state actors is not necessary to invoke the prohibitions on torture found in Art. 3 of each of the four Geneva Conventions of 1949, Mendez explains, giving an example that non-state actors such as armed groups can be reached under the law.[142] The question for purposes of our topic, thus, becomes, whether non-state actors who torture persons in the production of pornography, and those who possess or distribute such pornography, who are not involved in an armed conflict, can be prosecuted under international laws prohibiting torture.

CAT, art. 1 defines torture as

---

[140] *Ibid.*
[141] *Ibid.*, 256-257
[142] Mendez, 251

> Any act by which severe pain or suffering, whether physical or mental, is intentionally inflicted on a person for such purposes of obtaining from him or a third person information or a confession, punishing him for an act he or a third person has committed or is suspected of having committed, or intimidating or coercing him or a third person, or for any reason based on discrimination of any kind, when such pain or suffering is inflicted by or at the instigation of or with the consent or acquiescence of a public official or other person acting in an official capacity. It does not include pain or suffering arising only from, inherent in or incidental to lawful sanctions.[143]

I would also be concerned about pain or suffering arising from "lawful" sanctions because, as we know, such sanctions can cover torture such as the death penalty or deprivation of prisoner's rights or depriving prisoners of necessities of life such as proper food, water, exercise, health care, and more.

When violence against women is involved, it would be considered gender-specific

---

[143] Bisset, reprint of CAT, 76

discrimination, which would activate a state's obligation to prevent discriminatory acts (of torture and CIDT) according to Mendez.[144] Although it is not binding law, Mendez points out that the CAT General Comment 2, p. 18, obligates state authorities who have knowledge of or reasonable grounds to believe that acts prohibited by CAT are being done by non-state actors, and fail to "exercise due diligence" to investigate, prevent, prosecute, and punish such actors will be held responsible for such acts.[145] Mendez states that CAT has been invoked concerning gender-based violence such as domestic violence, rape, female genital mutilation and human trafficking.[146] Importantly, states are required to rehabilitate and offer reparations to victims of torture based on General Comment 3 to CAT which was enacted on December 13, 2012, he adds.[147] We posit that extreme hard-core pornography is a type of gender-based violence.

Jeanne Sarson and Linda MacDonald point out that torture is an intentional and deliberate act which dehumanizes its victims. They

---

[144] Mendez, 256
[145] *Ibid.*, 258
[146] *Ibid.*
[147] *Ibid.*, 261

believe that when state authorities are aware that non-state actors are torturing persons there is a duty to act under CAT. They mention that non-state actors to whom such a law could apply include pornographers, pimps, johns, human traffickers, pedophiles, parents and spouses.[148] The article details torture methods used against victims.[149]

Examples are provided by the group Non-State Torture:[150]

The Canadian Federation of University Women has called for Canada to criminalize torture by non-state actors.[151] The organization, Persons Against Nonstate Torture published a wheel describing the issue

---

[148] Jeanne Sarson and Linda MacDonald, 'Having Non-State Torture Recognized by the UN and Member States as an Infringement of Women's Human Rights is Imperative,' [2018] 33(1 & 2) Canadian Woman Studies/Les Cahrers De La Femme 144-146

[149] *Ibid.*, 148-151

[150] Jeanne Sarson and Linda MacDonald, 'Global NST Categories in the Private/Domestic Sphere,' Accessed Internet 28 June 2019 at
http://nonstatetorture.org/~nonstate/what-is-nst/non-state-torture

[151] Canadian Federation of University Women, "Non-State Actor Torture,' Accessed Internet 28
June 2019, at http://www.fcfdu.org/en-ca/whatwedo/advocacy/cfuwnationaladvocacypriorities/nationalinitiativeonviolenceagainstwomen.aspx

which readers can consult.[152] The fact sheet explaining the wheel emphasizes that non-state torture is a human rights crime and includes the trafficking of women and children "into sexualized exploitation---for prostitution and for pornographic victimizations."[153]

In my view, governments often are complicit in human rights violations committed by private persons or groups by failing to prevent the abuse, torture, or terrorism.

E. Torture as a Violation of ICCPR Article 7

Further support for the idea that torture and violent pornography are torture or other cruel, inhuman or degrading treatment in violation norms/customary international law is provided by its inclusion in one of the oldest and most strongly supported international human rights treaties---the International Covenant on Civil and Political Rights (1966). ICCPR Article 7 provides that "no one shall be

---

[152] Nonstate Torture Wheel, http://nonstatetorture.org/~nonstate/what-is-nst/non-state-torture, Accessed Internet 28 June 2019

[153] Jeanne Sarson and Linda MacDonald, 'The Non-State Torture (NST) Wheel: A Fact Sheet,' Accessed Internet 28 June 2019 at
http://nonstatetorture.org/~nonstate/application/files/7415/3694/3648/NSTwheelFACTSHEETkeepv2.pdf

subjected to torture or to cruel, inhuman or degrading treatment or punishment." Importantly, as Mickelwait explains, in its 1982 General Comment No 7, the Human Rights Committee opined that such punishment "need not be executed by a public official" to violate Art. 7.[154] This means that private persons and private organizations or companies acting without state authority can be found to violate this international treaty.

ICCPR Art. 19 allows freedom of speech to be restricted, only as provided by law "or necessary: a) For respect of the rights or reputation of others: b) For the protection of national security or of public order, or of public health or morals." We would argue that torture pornography, extreme and violent pornography, nonconsensual pornography, and image-based sexual abuse can be regulated by criminal and civil law because it concerns the reputation and rights of persons, and to protect public health or morals.

F. Torture and Degrading Treatment Under ECHR Art. 3

Art. 3 of the European Convention on Human Rights prohibits the "torture or

---

[154] Mickelwait, 1

inhuman or degrading treatment or punishment" of a person. Johnson points out that states are obligated, under this article, to act to prevent such treatment of persons in their jurisdiction. He believes that extreme pornography could be tackled in individual complaints made to the ECtHR under Art. 3 against states for failure to regulate such material.[155] Johnson suggests that a complaint could be filed claiming a state failed to take sufficient action to regulate the availability of certain types of pornographic images such as those involving rape or sexual violence, and that an Art. 3 degrading treatment case might be possible.[156]

The Johnson article demonstrates that pornography-related cases tending so show up before the ECtHR are those being filed by individuals who have been criminally charged with pornography offenses in their own countries and who seek to have their convictions overturned based on human rights law involving theories such as freedom of speech and privacy. In general this court tends

---

[155] Paul Johnson, 'Pornography and the European Convention on Human Rights,' [2014] 1(3) Porn Studies, 299, 314

[156] Johnson, 317

to give states a wide margin of appreciation to create and judge their own national laws on questions of morals (which pornography can be), particularly because, as the court said in the 1976 case of *Handyside v. United Kingdom* (1975) s. 48: "it is not possible to find in the domestic law of the various Contracting States a uniform European conception of morals."[157] Although the requirements of necessity (for the regulation) and proportionality (is the regulation proportionate to the severity of the offense) are looked at by the European court, the court tends to reject cases involving laws governing pornography and obscenity and leave those matters up to the individual states, Johnson demonstrates.[158] The widely divergent decisions of the court, as (detailed in Johnson, who provides a useful list of ECtHR cases involving pornography,[159]) regarding pornography regulation, create an uncertainty regarding the conflict between victims' rights and protection of health and morals and the free speech rights of pornographers.

Non-state torture needs to be criminalized internationally and in each nation state

---

[157] Johnson, 304
[158] *Ibid.*, 305
[159] *Ibid.*, 320

because of the horrific abuse victims of torture endure. This must include torture pornography.

Chapter Six: Shutting Down the Pornography Industry: Proposals for Change

A. Shut Down TOR Onion Router Or Have Nations Block Its Use

While working on other methods to remove pornography from the Internet, states can act to fulfil their due diligence obligations, at the present time, to remove the majority of child pornography, and presumably some adult extreme, violent, torture, nonconsensual, and IBSA pornography from the Internet by blocking or shutting down Tor, The Onion Router, and similar technology and blocking VPNs. Victims of pornography need this kind of action ASAP and cannot wait for the snail's pace of international treaties to be acted upon, especially considering that most contain no enforcement mechanisms. The only way to eliminate Dark Web crime would be to eliminate the Dark Web, Shillito suggests, recognizing it is more likely that states will use two other approaches: takedown of illegitimate sites and denying people access to the Dark Web.[160]

---

[160]Shillito, 198

The U.S. government's military developed the Internet technology (Tor) which enables organized crime to worldwide market and/or promote illicit and illegal goods including child pornography (and probably adult pornography, too), illegal drugs, illegal weapons, prostitution, trafficking in persons, and other questionable items on the Dark Web. The U.S. government then appears to be fighting said same traffic in goods and services by conducting and publicizing minor law enforcement efforts to shut down said sales. We call this The Cat Chasing Its Own Tail. If we correctly believe that the U.S. has enabled private parties to flood the Internet with child pornography it is then necessary for the human rights of victims of such pornography to obtain justice through one or more other nations willing to prosecute the U.S. under universal jurisdiction for failing to meet its obligations as a state to combat pornography.

The U.S. Navy developed Tor, a.k.a., The Onion Router. Tor enables people to remain anonymous on the Internet. This is great for governments conducting surveillance efforts, legitimate or not, isn't it? Amanda Haaz explains that the United States Navy created TOR to "make online communication untraceable and anonymous" and could use it to set up strings, seek anonymous tips, and "explore illegal sites without the owners learning of it."[161] Tor was invented by the U.S. Naval Research Laboratory and released for public use in 2004 as an open source project called Tor Project, Inc.[162] Developers Roger Dingledine and Nick Mathewson took over Tor as a private no longer military project in 2002.[163] Tor is partly sponsored by the U.S. government and other sponsors can be found here: https://www.torproject.org/about/sponsors.html.en[164]

Tor is promoted to the general public as a tool to be anonymous on the web with good purposes such as complaining about totalitarian governments, free speech, free press, freedom of association, protecting domestic violence victims from their abusers, and more. The availability of Tor as open source software enables anyone (at least in

---

[161] Amanda Haasz, 'Underneath it All: Policing International Child Pornography on the Dark Web,' [2016] 43(2) Syracuse J. Int'l L. & Com. 353, 358

[162] Abbott, 22

[163] *Ibid.*, 18
[164] White, et al., 67

most nations) to download it and use it to have their IP Internet addresses hidden from everyone, including law enforcement authorities. Use of Tor enables persons who use the Dark Web to be anonymous often with illicit and questionable intentions.

The availability of Tor enables the organized crime international industry/enterprise to create websites on the Dark Web where trading in illegal and illicit items and services occurs. In developing and enabling the widespread use of Tor among the general public and organized criminals, the U.S. government is deliberately allowing illegal items and services to flourish on the Dark Web, including pornography (including child pornography), the topic of this dissertation.

1. What is Tor Onion Router?

The Onion Router (Tor) is "a proxy that masks the location information and browsing history of the user, allowing for anonymous use of the Internet" working through a network of relays which "encrypt the original user's traffic so that the location information cannot be discovered."[165] Cleverly, no one authority controls the Tor Network.[166]

2. What Are Good and Bad (Criminal) Uses of Tor?

Some see Tor as being an important tool for human rights, privacy, intellectual freedom and speech, and combatting domestic violence stalkers.[167] However, a study by Guitton [2013] found that hidden services are not being used as a place to discuss politics to try to find better democratic options than existing states and that what showed up prominently was child pornography and illegal drugs.[168]

White, et al. state: ". . . behind the layers of the onion lies the traditional criminal enterprise. Investigators should be cognizant of the fact that accessing the darknet is simply

---

[165] Alison Macrina and Eric Phetteplace, 'The Tor Browser and Intellectual Freedom in the Digital Age,' [Summer 2015] 54(4) Reference & User Services Quarterly 17, 18

[166] Richard Abbott, 'An Onion A Day Keeps the NSA Away,' [2010] J. of Internet Law 22

[167] Macrina and Phetteplace, 18

[168] Clement Guitton, 'A Review of Available Content On Tor Hidden Services:The Case Against Further Development,' [2013] 29 Computers in Human Behavior 2805, 2809, 2810

one component of the new criminal enterprise.[169]

By using a Virtual Private Network (VPN) with Tor, for encryption and security, criminals can potentially "anonymously conduct cross-border crime. . . ."[170] Shillito (2019) states that it is believed that at least 50 percent of what Tor hosts is "illegal and illegitimate."[171] Marketplaces on the Dark Web are reached through their .onion address and operate "like an eBay for illicit goods."[172] The goods and services traded on the Dark Web include child pornography, hitmen, illegal drugs, fake IDs, firearms, and more.[173] Cryptocurrencies such as Bitcoin, Monero, Ethereum, and Lite coin, which hide their original source, are used to transact business on the Dark Web, adding

---

[169] White, et al., 71
[170] Matthew Robert Shillito, 'Untangling the "Dark Web": An Emerging Technological Challenge for the Criminal Law,' [2019] 28:2 Infor. & Communications Tech. L. 186, 187

[171] Shillito, 190
[172] Shillito, 190
[173] Shillito, 190

more anonymity to transactions according to U.S. attorneys.[174]

3. Dark Web Takedowns

The surface web contains items indexed by a standard search engine such as Yahoo or Google. IP addresses of users of the surface web are traceable which is how search engines use cookies to promote products to us which we might be interested in. We can find millions of listings leading to extreme adult pornography on such search engines (and we would argue that these intermediaries who enable such websites to be located by pornography consumers should be held accountable when and where laws against pornography exist). Surface web searches can lead to deep web sites (such as a government grants site). Lastly, the Dark Web is a part of the Deep Web which is hidden and can only be accessed by special web browsers such as TOR, The Onion Router which protects the anonymity of the user by "pinging his/her Internet Protocol ("IP")

---

[174]Ryan White, Puneet V. Kakkar and Vicki Chou, 'Prosecuting Darknet Marketplaces: Challenges and Approaches,' [2019] 67 U.S. Att'ys Bull. 65, 66, 68

address randomly from place to place so the user's activities are less traceable."[175]

Silk Road, accessible only through the Tor network, was known as the eBay of the Dark Web and was where persons bought and sold goods anonymously for Bitcoins (anonymous currency), with most items being illegal such as child pornography, illegal drugs, hit men, weapons, and document forgeries.[176] The FBI took down Silk Road and a large host of child porn called Freedom Hosting, according to Haasz, but images remained available because they were backed up on another Freedom Hosting server called Lolita City.[177] Haasz concludes that the Dark Web would have to be gotten rid of in order to eliminate child pornography on the Dark Web.[178]

4. Attempts to Block the Dark Web or Tor

Shillito notes that China and Turkey blocked access to Tor by having ISPs (internet service providers) "revoke access to the Tor network" but some users got around that by using VPNs to look like they, as users, are from different

---

[175] Haasz, 357
[176] *Ibid.*, 358
[177] *Ibid.*, 374
[178] *Ibid.*, 378

nations. This resulted in China and Russia trying to block VPNs.[179] Blocking can be avoided by using an exit node in a nation that is not blocking a website that is blocked in the nation one is located in, Abbott explains.[180] Watson writes about the efforts of China, Saudia Arabia, and the United Arab Emirates to filter Tor. China requires people to go through government channels to access the internet and censors content, and has laws making it illegal to produce or disseminate obscene or pornographic materials.[181] Users, however are able to frustrate the China firewall by routing internet traffic through exit nodes in other nations.[182] Saudi Arabia also routes all traffic through its government network and filters sites which feature pornography.[183]

In my view, these efforts to block Tor and to block VPNs are an example of nations exercising their obligations as states under international treaties which can be interpreted

---

[179]Shillito, 198-199
[180]Abbott, 24
[181]Watson, 727, fn. 59
[182]Ibid., 728
[183]Ibid., 729

to require eliminating pornography and using due diligence.

Interestingly, Wikipedia has blocked Tor users from posting or editing material on its site through Tor.[184]

Skorzewska-Amberg states that some nations have blocked access to content containing child pornography by using "filter or in combination with lists of illegal addresses."[185] While the best solution, in her view, would be to eliminate sites which have child pornography, this can only be done if a server is in the country whose jurisdiction allows such site elimination, she states.[186] There are also concerns that sites which do not contain anything illegal could be blocked, and a proper balance between the rule of law guarantees and citizens' rights guarantees must be maintained, she explains.[187]

Binford, et al. report that technology can be used to reduce victimization. They state that technology is being developed which "can quickly identify child pornography and remove

---

[184] Abbott, 27
[185] Skorzewska-Amberg, 269-270
[186] *Ibid.*, 270
[187] *Ibid.*

it from the Internet" thus reducing access.[188] They state:

> Twitter, Facebook, Microsoft, and Google have already implemented software known at PhotoDNA that can quickly identify child pornography, allowing the companies to report the possessor to authorities.[189] Search engines can report such pornography and block it from a search result.[190] I find it disturbing that they do not also remove the child pornography from the web.

A digital forensics tool suite named Artemis was developed by the Oak Ridge National Laboratory, the University of North Carolina at Wilmington and the Knoxville, Tennessee Police Department.[191] Ricarnek and Boehnen report that Artemis "combines facial analytics with other technologies to quickly scan

---

[188] Binford, et al., 128

[189] *Ibid.*, 129 (sources omitted)

[190] *Ibid.*

[191] Karl Ricanek Jr. and Chris Boehnen, 'Facial Analytics: From Big Data To Law Enforcement,' accessed, Internet 13 July 2019, https://www.researchgate.net/publication/25801914 Doi: 10.1109/MC.2012.308, 96

computers and memory devices for child pornography" and note that it would usually take a forensic examiner two to five days to search a home computer for child pornography and write a report.[192] Artemis also generates a forensics report including photos which are tagged, enabling law enforcement to follow up and arrest perpetrators and rescue children, they state.[193] PhotoDNA (developed by Microsoft) is integrated into the Artemis technology, they explain, noting that it also uses a "facial analytics engine" which was developed by the Institute for Interdisciplinary Studies and the Face Aging Group to determine whether an image is of a child or an adult, and to extract demographic data.[194]

5. Conclusion

Shillito mentions that the "powerful nation state" of the U.S. has tried to set the agenda regarding regulating the Dark Web, for example, by either leading or assisting "in all major Dark Web takedowns to date."[195] An example of this is the Silk Road takedown and

---

[192] *Ibid.*
[193] *Ibid.*, 96-97
[194] *Ibid.*, 98
[195] Shillito, 196-197

the case against its owner, *U.S. v. Ross William Ulbricht*.[196] Shillito states that the U.S. is preoccupied with "reducing drug-related crime", including on the Dark Web, reminding us that it is important "that international efforts do not overlook Dark Web crimes such as the sale of firearms or the selling of child pornography . . . ."[197]

We conclude that it is up to other nation states to use universal jurisdiction to fulfil their obligations to act to shut down the pornography industry on the Internet.

B. Other Recommended Actions

1. Amend Current Human Rights Treaties

Current treaties such as ICCPR, CEDAW, and CAT should be amended to specifically require states to ban extreme, violent, IBSA, and nonconsensual pornography (defined as suggested herein) and to specify that victim of such pornography can sue for damages in civil courts. A common definition of pornography should be included in such instruments.

The definition of crimes against humanity in the Rome Statute of the ICC should be

---

[196] *U.S. v. Ross William Ulbricht*, 31 F. Supp. 3d 540 (2014)
[197] Shillito, 197

amended to specify that it includes such pornography.

2. Enforcement Issues

A way to enforce the decisions of human rights regional courts and of the international treaty committees and commissions must be found and added to international law. Perhaps insight can be gained from examining how enforcement is maintained in international civil arenas such as trade law, banking, air space, maritime law, labor laws, nuclear arms treaties, arbitration law, and laws governing aspects of the environment. If various laws and customs are regularly applied to cover such matters, why can't the world find effective ways to protect human rights?

C. Creation of An International Cybercrime Convention/Treaty

In reality, we can create all the international, regional, and national anti-pornography laws we can design, but if the laws are not used or enforced, we have failed at our goal of protecting victims of pornography-related crimes. As Shytov states, "In order to suppress pornography one has to win the technological battle through blocking pornographic materials."[198]

In order to regulate something on the Internet, it would have to be illegal under either international or national laws. That, of course, includes pornography in all its forms. Our argument is that international treaties and customary law require states to ban child pornography and IBSA, extreme, violent, nonconsensual types of pornography under their obligations as states. Under an international cybercrime convention, the crimes would most likely have to be defined as international crimes meaning common definitions and regulations and punishments would need to be created covering each crime topic. It is possible to do this. The Rome Statue of the ICC, for example, created internationally applicable crimes, with detailed definitions, covering genocide, war crimes, crimes of aggression, and crimes against humanity. Any international crimes would have to be investigated and prosecuted at the international level, either by the ICC by extending the jurisdiction of the crimes it

---

[198]Shytov, 279

covers, or by the creation of an International Cybercrimes Court.

In addition to dealing with adult extreme pornography and child pornography, an international cybercrime convention could greatly help hold cyber-criminals accountable for other crimes which cross national borders such as trafficking in persons, drug trafficking, computer crimes, weapons trade, money laundering, racketeering, terrorism, identify theft, and more, I believe. Therefore, I propose that an international cybercrime convention be enacted to cover those and other cross-border crimes.

Cameron S.D. Brown posits that the main reasons why investigations and prosecutions of cybercrimes often do not get done are because of
"trans-jurisdictional barriers, subterfuge and the inability of key stakeholders in the criminal justice systems to grasp fundamental aspects of technology aided crime."[199] For example skilled investigators knowledgeable about internet

---

[199] Cameron S.D. Brown, 'Investigating and Prosecuting Cyber Crime: Forensic Dependencies and Barriers to Justice,' [January- June 2015] 9(1) Int'l J. of Cyber Criminology 55, 56

technology are needed to effectively investigate and gather evidence of cyber-crimes and police agencies must have the funding to conduct such complex investigations.[200] Differences in legal systems across the globe as well as advances in information communication technologies (ICTs) also impede cyber-crime enforcement efforts.[201]

Existing law enforcement limits the ability of authorities to tackle Dark Web cybercrime, including pornography. Organizations like Interpol and Europol collect information and coordinate sharing that information with various nations and promote international and/or regional cooperation. However, they do not have the power to make laws or to enforce laws.[202] Unfortunately, Dark Web crimes often have cross-border elements which raise jurisdictional problems among states.[203]

1. Trans-border Elements of Cyber Crimes

Evidence, victims, and perpetrators of cybercrimes are often located in different nation states, Brown points out. It is difficult

---

[200] *Ibid.*, 64
[201] *Ibid.*, 56
[202] Shillito, 194
[203] Shillito, 195

to access cybercrime information stored in a different country. Such crimes are also often anonymous, making it harder to identify those responsible.[204] Identifying victims and perpetrators of cybercrimes can be difficult, and victims may not bring such crimes to the attention of law enforcement because they fear publicity or feel the incidents are not serious enough to report.[205] In addition, police agencies have often not considered fighting cybercrime a priority, Brown suggests.[206] One main reason that police are unable to take action against internet crimes is because they are unable to prove who the perpetrators in such crimes are.[207] In a Swedish study, police reported that the main reason for such an inability was because the ISPs and social media, many of which were foreign and outside their jurisdiction, which held that information refused to provide police with the information.[208]

---

[204] *Ibid.,* 58
[205] *Ibid.,* 59
[206] *Ibid.,* 63
[207] Bjarnadottir, 212
[208] *Ibid.,* citing *Polisanmalda brott hot och krankningar mot enskilda personer via internet.* Rapport 2015:6. "The study is accessible in Swedish with an English summary via the

2. Jurisdiction Issues

A cybercrime might be initiated in one legal jurisdiction (for example, one nation) but have its impact felt in a different jurisdiction (nation). The issue of which law enforcement agency has authority to investigate such a crime and pursue charges becomes a major consideration and potential roadblock to action.[209] For example, a pornography producer might film a rape of a woman in one country, distribute the film of the sexual assault by uploading it on the web in a different nation, and then the film would be seen in numerous other nations.[210] I would suggest that many nonconsensual pornography photos and films of children or adults could end up being seen in numerous different nations around the globe which further complicates the problem of how, and where to hold the criminal(s) involved in the rape and the production and distribution of the pornography accountable for their wrongful

---

Council's website at: <https://bra.se/5.5e2a4a6b166759983d.html#>

[209] *Ibid.*, 62

[210] Amanda Haasz, 'Underneath it All: Policing International Child Pornography on the Dark Web,' [2016] 43(2) Syracuse J. Int'l L. & Com. 353, 354

acts. This is also an issue when a victim of pornography wishes to go after those involved in a civil case which could involve assault and battery, copyright violations, defamation, invasion of privacy, loss of work, intentional infliction of emotional distress, loss of friendships and co-workers, and physical or mental illness. Which nation's laws apply to such a civil case? What, if anything, can be done to prevent the pornography from continuing to be shared across the web?

The U.S. DOJ states, on its website, that federal jurisdiction applies to child pornography situations in interstate or foreign commerce. It explains that foreign commerce is "almost always" involved when a child pornography case involves the Internet. Persons outside the U.S. are not allowed to "knowingly produce, receive, transport, ship, or distribute child pornography with intent to import or transmit the visual depiction into the United States" under 18 U.S.C. S. 2260.[211] Greek criminal law provides that Internet offenses involving access in Greek territories

---

[211] United States Department of Justice, https://www.justice.gov/criminal-ceos/citizens-guide-us-federal-law-child-pornography, Accessed, Internet, 10 August 2019

"are considered to have been committed in the Greek territory" no matter where they are hosted.[212]

3. Should Intermediaries Be Criminally Liable?

The most effective remedy, Suzor, Seignior, and Singleton believe would be to tackle the pornography issue at the most "effective points of control"---namely, through the "intermediaries who host, index and make available content . . . ." This includes those who provide telecommunications, social media platforms, search engines, and network hosts. Reducing visibility of the materials in question can be accomplished by making certain that name searches of victims do not result in prominently featured intimate images, making certain that such materials are not spread in popular and relevant social networks, and regulating "the most influential sites that host and distribute content online."[213] Intermediaries, in our view, should not have immunity. Danielle Keats Citron, in her book *Hate Crimes in Cyberspace*, states she would not permit websites or content hosts which

---

[212]Dimoulas, et al., 8
[213]Suzor, et al., 1066-1067

host nonconsensual pornography or cyberstalking or which seek financial gain from removing such materials, to be immune from criminal or civil liability.[214] We point out, however, that monitoring, by intermediaries, of content posted by websites might be cost prohibitive and would involve being very judgmental about which content violates laws against pornography. Once notified by victims or law enforcement that content on their search engines, for example, is criminal, or civilly actionable, such hosts should have procedures in place to remove such content from the Internet or be held criminally and civilly liable for such postings. Websites, in our view, should clearly be held responsible for content posted on them.

Suzor, et al. emphasize that it would be costly in terms of finances and social costs to freedom of expression and highly prohibitive for internet intermediaries to monitor content.[215] We note that, in international human rights law, such a balancing act is often done by courts between individual rights such

---

[214] Danielle Keats Citron, *Hate Crimes in Cyberspace* [2014] Cambridge, MA: Harvard University Press, 177
[215] *Ibid.*, 1069, 1071

as privacy vs. individual rights of freedom of expression and association.

Akdeniz (2009) states that ISPs are ordinarily, under the law, liable for distributing child pornography if they have knowledge and control over the information being transmitted or stored.[216] ISPs are necessary to access the Internet, but they do not control third-party content, Akdeniz notes. It would be impossible, therefore, for a single ISP to "control, monitor or judge" the huge amount of Internet content and whether there is illegal activity going on.[217] There have been prosecutions of CompuServe in Germany for assisting in distributing child pornography, and against Yahoo in France regarding anti-Semitism.[218]

4. Websites Refusing to Share Information with Authorities and Other

Law Enforcement Issues

Combatting cyber pornography creates huge problems for law enforcement authorities.

---

[216] Yaman Akdeniz, *Internet Child Pornography and the Law National and International Responses* [2008, 2009] Farnham, Surrey: Ashgate Publishing, Ltd., 12

[217] *Ibid.*, 227-229
[218] *Ibid.*, 229-231

There is, first and foremost, the problem of jurisdiction (discussed elsewhere). Bjarnadottir explains that police encounter problems with foreign ISP's, social media, and websites refusing to share information with them about whom the distributor/perpetrator of the cyber pornography is.[219] We add that it is a complex legal situation to have to obtain authority to obtain such information through methods of search and seizure, especially when more than one nation is involved and each nation's laws regarding obtaining such data differ. Search and seizure issues also involve which state's laws on that topic apply and making certain that defendant rights not to be subjected to illegal searches and seizures, to due process, and to rule of law application are upheld. According to Binford, et. al., "many smartphones contain security that prevents law enforcement from accessing data, making a smartphone an ideal medium for perpetrators."[220]

---

[219] Maria Run Bjarnadottir, 'Does the Internet Limit Human Rights Protection? The Case of Revenge Porn,' [2016] 7(3) J. of Intellectual Property, Information Technology and E-Commerce Law 204-215, 212

[220] Binford, et. al., 124, citing Craig Timberg and Greg Miller, 'FBI Blasts Apple, Google for Locking Police Out of Phones,' [25 September 2014] *Wash. Post.* Available at

5. Inclusion of Pornography Crimes In A Cybercrime Convention

If these types of pornography are not considered a crime against humanity under the Rome Statute of the ICC, the jurisdiction of crimes under the ICC needs to be expanded to cover such pornography and define it as an international crime including with enforcement and penalties. Special laws and procedures may be advisable to deal with the problem of minors who "sext" pornographic photos of themselves or their friends due to their juvenile status.

We ask: Why not create such a criminal law at the international level which would bind all parties who sign and ratify the law? Approaching this internationally would enable the reality that extreme and violent, nonconsensual, image based sexual abuse, and child pornography often cross borders and raise jurisdiction issues. The international law would also have to include provisions enabling victims to file civil lawsuits for damages against

---

http://www.washingtonpost.com/business/technology/2014/09/25/68c4e08e-4344-11e4-9a15-137aa015327_story.html

the producers, distributors and sharers of the pornography at issue. These laws would be required to be enacted and enforced in the nations under such a treaty. States would also be required to enact and enforce such laws in their national laws.

Kalim, in 2013, proposed that a single international law be created to combat child pornography. He states that problems with the existing approach include the inability to agree on the age of consent (13 to 21), the inability of some developing nations to measure the use of the internet and identify online sex offenders, and the fact that there is no governing body in existence to police child pornography, making it hard to measure.[221]

6. Creation of a Law Enforcement Agency, A Prosecutorial and Defense

Division and A Cybercrime Court

The next question becomes, who will enforce such a treaty?

I propose that an international law enforcement division be created under an

---

[221] Alexander Kalim, 'Addressing The Gap in International Instruments Governing Internet Child Pornography,' [2013] 21 Common Law Conspectus, 428, 429-436

international cybercrimes treaty to investigate such crimes and with police powers to arrest suspects/those accused. This law enforcement agency would have to have appropriate access to information, in all the nations, relating to each particular crime and the ability to conduct investigations, obtain evidence, interview witnesses, and do searches and seizures in the nation(s) at issue. A separate division should be created to bring criminal charges and prosecute such crime and include a victims' advocacy branch (similar to that of the ICC). Another division would be created to defend those accused and ensure that the human rights, and due process rights of defendants are not violated. A third division (trial and appellate court) should be created to judge the guilt or innocence of those accused of cybercrimes which could be called the International Cybercrimes Court. The pornography crimes created under the cybercrimes convention would be one area of many crimes handled by these new agencies and court.

D. Creation of An International Human Rights Court

One proposal the former CEDAW Committee Chair Dubravka Simonovic is aware of is "the need for a permanent body to deal with complaints that arise under CEDAW Convention and other UN Conventions by establishing a permanent UN Human Rights Court."[222] She states that the first step could involve organizing the work of all the treaty bodies "with a complaint and inquiry system that would increase the interaction and consistency of the treaty bodies' work."[223] This could evolve into a Human Rights Court or a Complaints and Inquiries System with petitions and inquiries handled in the OHCHR, she suggests.[224]

Creation of such investigating/prosecuting/defending and judicial bodies should probably involve jurisdiction over all international human rights laws and enable individuals to also file complaints. This could best be done through creation of an international human rights court. Criminal aspects of wrongdoing involving international human rights could be handled by a law enforcement investigating agency and prosecuting agency within the

---

[222]Simonovic, 598
[223]*Ibid.*, 598-599
[224]*Ibid.*, 599

divisions of such a court, and civil matters could be handled by a civil division. There would have to be a way for court judgments to be enforced against defendants who are convicted in criminal cases or found at fault in civil cases. Here again, the principle of subsidiarity and sovereignty would give individual nations the first chance to adequately handle the alleged human rights violations with jurisdiction passing to the International Human Rights Court upon failure of a state to appropriately act. We believe such a court would be a good way to ensure that international human rights treaties and rights of individuals under them are enforced.

Conclusion

Violence against women and girls in the world is primarily gendered (committed by males against females), making it an issue of discrimination, hatred/misogyny, lack of freedom, and inequality. Pornography is just one of the means used to promote violence against women and it involves crimes of violence against women in its production. Women also face, in huge numbers, domestic violence, rape, war rape, female genital mutilation, forced pregnancy, femicide and honor crimes, trafficking in persons, prostitution, sterilization, hate crimes, genocide, and crimes against humanity. Why is our world tolerating such violence toward one-half of its population? What is causing males to treat women this way? How can the demand for these abusive acts be eliminated? We do not address these issues in this paper but raise the question for consideration among the international community.

The governments we are attempting to rely upon to enforce laws against violence against women are a major part of the problem. As Dauer states:

Violence continues because governments may implicitly condone it, ignoring acts of violence in the family and community, thus allowing impunity to be the norm and preventing women from achieving equality in political, economic, and social life. Consistent lack of accountability for violence against women creates a climate in which these acts are seen as normal and acceptable.[225] An idea to create a new treaty, a convention on violence against women, was abandoned by the UN Commission on the Status of Women.[226]

A wide variety of civil lawsuit possibilities exist, in individual nations, for survivors of sexual abuse, including of pornography-related harms, to use to obtain damages and reparation for their injuries and harms. These have not been addressed here but have been addressed at length in my 1989 book, *Sourcebook On Pornography*. These legal theories include assault, battery, negligence, intentional infliction of emotional distress, negligent infliction of emotional distress, defamation, invasion of privacy, copyright

---

[225]Dauer, 2
[226]Simonovic, 600

violations, injunctive relief, sex discrimination, sexual harassment, stalking, laws prohibiting revenge pornography, civil organized crime and racketeering claims, strict products liability, and the right to be forgotten theory. Civil remedies are extremely important because they can provide the means to make pornography production and dissemination non-profitable, which would cause the industry to cease such activities. Transnational issues, jurisdiction matters, and problems identifying those responsible for particular pornography being on the Internet plague criminal and civil cases.

It is important to emphasize that it is generally a whole lot cheaper for governments and societies to prevent crimes and human rights violations before they occur than it is to cure the problems (medical, psychological, community-wise, economic, social, other) caused by such crimes and violations.

Ultimately, we have demonstrated that, for the most part, little is being done internationally, to get child pornography and adult extreme pornography off the Internet. The ICCPR, Art. 2(3)(a), CAT Art. 14, the Optional Protocol to CRC, Art. 9(4), and the Palermo Protocol (concerning human trafficking) Art. 6, for example, require state parties to provide an effective remedy to persons whose freedoms or rights have been violated.[227] States are not complying with their obligations as states to get pornography off the Internet and to provide remedies to persons whose rights have been violated. No authority exists to force states to comply with their obligations. We can therefore conclude that, *Ubi jus ibi remedium:* a right without a remedy is no right at all.

---

[227] ECPAT, 'Barriers to Compensation for Child Victims of Sexual Exploitation,' [2016], 11-12

Bibliography

Richard Abbott, 'An Onion A Day Keeps the NSA Away,' [2010] J. of Internet Law 22

Yaman Akdeniz, *Internet Child Pornography and the Law National and International Responses* [2008, 2009] Farnham, Surrey: Ashgate Publishing, Ltd.

Rabia Akhtar, 'The Neglected Boys of War: Trapped In A Vicious Cycle of Slavery and Sexual Abuse,' [2019] 3 J. of Traff. And Human Exploitation 179, 186-187

Axelle Apvrille, 'The Evolution of Mobile Malware,' [August 2014] Computer Fraud & Security 18

Warren Binford, 'A Global Survey of Country Efforts to Ensure Compensation for Child Pornography Victims,' [2015] 13(1) Ohio State J. of Crim. L. 37

Warren Binford, Janna Giesbrecht-McKee, Joshua L. Savey and Rachel Schwartz-Gilbert, 'Beyond Paroline: Ensuring Meaningful Remedies for Child Pornography Victims at Home and Abroad,' [2015] 35 Child. Legal Rts. J. 117

Maria Run Bjarnadottir, 'Does the Internet Limit Human Rights Protection? The Case of Revenge Porn,' [2016] 7(3) J. of Intellectual Property, Information Technology and E-Commerce Law 204-215

Cameron S.D. Brown, 'Investigating and Prosecuting Cyber Crime: Forensic Dependencies and Barriers to Justice,' [January- June 2015] 9(1) Int'l J. of Cyber Criminology 55

Elie Bursztein, Travis Bright, Einat Clarke, Michelle DeLaune, David M. Elifff, Nick Hsu, Lindsey Olson, John Shehan, Madhukar Thakur, Kurt Thomas. 2019. Rethinking the Detection of Child Sexual Abuse Imagery on the Internet. In Proceedings of the 2019 World Wide Web Conference

(WWW '19), May 13–17, 2019, San Francisco, CA, USA. ACM, New York NY, USA, 7 pages. https://doi.org/10.1145/3308558.3313482

Meghan Campbell, 'Women's Rights and the Convention on the Elimination of all Forms of Discrimination Against Women: Unlocking the Potential of the Optional Protocol,' [2016] Nordic Journal of Human Rights, 34:4, 247-271

Canadian Federation of University Women, "Non-State Actor Torture,' Accessed Internet 28 June 2019, at http://www.fcfdu.org/en-ca/whatwedo/advocacy/cfuwnationaladvocacypriorities/nationalinitiativeonviolenceagainstwomen.aspx

Paul Cesarini, 'Caught in the Network,' [2007] 53(23) Chron. Of Higher Ed. B5

Lura Chamberlain, 'FOSTA: A Hostile Law with a Human Cost,' [2019] 87 Fordham L. Rev. 2171

Christine Chinkin, 'Addressing violence against women in the Commonwealth within states' obligations under international law,' [2014] Commonwealth Law Bulletin, 40:3, 471-501

D. Keats Citron, *Hate Crimes in Cyberspace* [2014] Harvard University Press. Cambridge, Massachusetts

Antonio Coco, 'The Universal Duty to Establish Jurisdiction over, and Investigate, Crimes Against Humanity: Preliminary Remarks on Draft Articles 7, 8, 9 and 11 by the International Law Commission,' [2018] 16 J. of Int'l Crim. J. 751

Criminal Justice and Immigration Act 2008, 2008 c. 4, Part 5, Pornography, etc., Section 63, Accessed Internet 11 June 2019 at http://www.legislation.gov.uk/ukpga/2008/4/section/63

The Crown Prosecution Service, 'The Code for Crown Prosecutors: Legal Guidance, Extreme Pornography,' Accessed Internet 11 June 2019 at https://www.cps.gov.uk/legal-guidance/extreme-pornography

Sheila Dauer, 'Human Rights Responses to Violence Against Women,'[2019] in N. Reilly (ed), *International Human Rights of Women*, Springer, Singapore, 2019, 5

Walter DeKeseredy, 'Critical Criminological Understandings of Adult Pornography and Woman Abuse: New Progressive Directions in Research and Theory,' [2015] 4(4) IJCJ&SD 4

Walter S. DeKeserdy and Amanda Hallo-Sanchez, 'Adult Pornography and Violence Against Women in the Heartland: Results from a Rural Southeast Ohio Study,' [2016] Violence Against Women, 1-20

Sara De Vido, 'The Ratification of the Council of Europe Istanbul Convention by the EU: A Step Forward in the Protection of Women from Violence in the European Legal System,' [2017] 9(2) Eur. J. of Legal Studies 69

Vasilis Dimoulas, Maria Karagianni, Eugenia Patroni, and Lampros Tsogkas, 'Child Pornography In A Cloud Era,' [2018] THEMIS Competition 2018, Semi Final A- International Cooperation in Criminal Matters, National School of Judges

Claire P. Donohue, 'A Feminist Framing of Non-Consensual Pornography,' [2017] 17 U. Md. L. J. Race, Religion, Gender & Class 247

Andrea Dworkin and Catherine A. MacKinnon, *Pornography And Civil Rights: A New Day for Women's Equality* [1988]

Susan Easton, 'Criminalizing the Possession of Extreme Pornography: Sword or Shield?' [2011] 75 JCL 391-413

ECPAT, 'Barriers to Compensation for Child Victims of Sexual Exploitation,' [2016] European Court of Human Rights, 'Research Report: Child Sexual Abuse and Child Pornography in the Court's Case-Law,' [2011]

Elizabeth Kirby Fuller, 'Holding Producers and Distributors Liable for the Harms of Sexually Violent Pornography through Tort Law,' [1994] 5 Fordham Intell. Prop. Media & Ent. L. J. 125

Claudia Giunta, 'International Human Rights Standards on Sexual Violence against Women as They

Apply to Pornography,' [1997] *LLM Theses and Essays.* 196. https://digitalcommons.law.uga.edu/stu_llm/196 Accessed Internet 19 July 2019

Lisa Grans, 'The Istanbul Convention and the Positive Obligation to Prevent Violence,' [2018] 18 Human Rights L. Rev. 133

Clement Guitton, 'A Review of Available Content On Tor Hidden Services: The Case Against Further Development,' [2013] 29 Computers in Human Behavior 2805

Amanda Haasz, 'Underneath it All: Policing International Child Pornography on the Dark Web,' [2016] 43(2) Syracuse J. Int'l L. & Com. 353

Haley Halverson, 'United Nations Special Rapporteur on Torture Report: The Gender-Based Torture Found in the Pornography Industry. The National Center on Sexual Exploitation. Accessed Internet 15 June 2019

Susan Hennessey, 'A Hoover Institution Essay: The Elephant in the Room: Addressing Child Exploitation and Going Dark,' [2017] Board of Trustees of the Leland Stanford Junior University, Hoover Institution

Tatjana Hornle and Mordechai Kremnitzer, 'Human Dignity As A Protected Interest In Criminal Law,' [2011] 44 Israel L. Rev. 143

Joel Hruska, 'Russia Might Ban Tor and Virtual Private Networks,' [13 February 2015] Extremetech.com

International Rehabilitation Council for Torture Victims, 'Rehabilitation of Torture Victims,' Accessed Internet 28 June 2019 at https://irct.org/what-we-do/rehabilitation-of-torture-victims

Danielle Ireland-Piper, 'Prosecutions of Extraterritorial Criminal Conduct and the Abuse of Rights Doctrine,' [2013] 9(4) Utrecht L. Rev. 68

Sara Lee Johann, *Sourcebook On Pornography* [1989] Lexington, MA: Lexington Books

Sara Johann, *Domestic Abusers: Terrorists In Our Homes* [1994] Springfield, IL: Charles C. Thomas, Publisher

Sara Johann, *Stop Domestic Violence* [2012] Light Shadows Communications, LLC

Paul Johnson, 'Pornography and the European Convention on Human Rights,' [2014] 1(3) Porn Studies, 299-320

Joshua H. Joseph, 'Gender and International Law: How the International Criminal Court Can Bring Justice to Victims of Sexual Violence,' [2008] 18 Tex. J. Women & L. 61

Mudasir Kamal and William J. Newman, 'Analysis and Commentary: Revenge Pornography: Mental Health Implications and Related Legislation,' [2016] 44(3) J. Am. Acad. Psychiatry Law 359

Robert Koch, Mario Golling and Gabi Dreo Rodosek, 'How Anonymous Is the Tor Network? A Long-Term Black-Box Investigation,' [2016] Computer 42

Maximo Langer, 'Universal Jurisdiction is Not Disappearing,' [2015] 13 J. of Int'l Crim. J., 245

Amanda Levendowski, 'Using Copyright to Combat Revenge Porn,' [2014] 3 N.Y.U.J. Intell. Prop. & Ent. L. 422

Catharine A. MacKinnon, 'Pornography as Trafficking,' [2005] 26(4) Mich. J. of Int'l Law 993

Alison Macrina and Eric Phetteplace, 'The Tor Browser and Intellectual Freedom in the Digital Age,' [Summer 2015] 54(4) Reference & User Services Quarterly 17

Sophie Maddocks, 'From Non-consensual Pornography to Image-based Sexual Abuse: Charting the Course of a Problem with Many Names,' [2018] 33:97Australian Feminist Studies 345-361

Jean-Baptiste Maillart, 'The Limits of Subjective Territorial Jurisdiction in the Context of Cybercrime,' [2019] 19 ERA Forum 375

Farhad Malekian, 'Trafficking in Persons and Pornography,' in Farhad Malekian, *Principles of Islamic International Criminal Law* [2011] Brill

Farhad Malekian and Kerstin Nordlof, *Prohibition of Sexual Exploitation of Children Constituting Obligation Erga* Omnes. [2013] Newcastle upon Tyne: Cambridge Scholars Publishing

Isabel Marcus, '"Reframing 'Domestic Violence": Terrorism in the Home,' in Martha Albertson Fineman and Roxanne Mykitiuk, eds., *The Public Nature of Private Violence: The Discovery of Domestic Abuse*. (London: Routledge, 1994) 25-26.

Clare McGlynn and Erika Rackley, 'Criminalising Extreme Pornography: lessons from England & Wales', [2013] Durham Law School Briefing Document, Durham University Accessed Internet 11 June 2019 https://www.dur.ac.uk/resources/glad/CMcGERExtremeP ornographyBriefingPaper.pdf

Juan E. Mendez, 'How International Law Can Eradicate Torture: A Response To Cynics,' [2016] 22 Southwestern J. of Int'l L. 247

Laila Mickelwait, 'BDSM Torture Porn and the law,' [18 August 2017] The New Jurist, 1, Accessed Internet 16 July 2019.

A.R. Mubarak, 'Child Safety Issues in Cyberspace: A Critical Theory on Trends and Challenges in the ASEAN Region,' [November 2015] 129 (1) Int'l J. of Computer Applications, 48

Abhilash Nair and James Griffin, 'The Regulation of Online Extreme Pornography: Purposive Teleology (in) Action,' [2013] 21(4) Int'l J. of Law and Information Technology 329

Natalie Nenadic, 'Genocide and Sexual Atrocities: Hannah Arendt's Eichmann in Jerusalem and Karadzic in New York,' [2011] 39(2) Philosophical Topics 117

Frida Nilsson, 'The Balance Between Patriarchal Oppression and Sexual Freedom: A Human Rights Based Approach to Pornography,' [2009] Paper presented in Human Rights Studies at Lunds Universitet

Dalsi Otero, 'Confronting Nonconsensual Pornography with Federal Criminalization and a Notice-and-Takedown Provision,' [2016] 70 U. Miami L. Rev. 585

Melanie Randall and Vasanthi Venkatesh, 'Symposium On The International Legal Obligation To Criminalize Marital Rape Criminalizing Sexual Violence Against Women In Intimate Relationships: State Obligations Under Human Rights Law,' [2016] 109 AJIL Unbound 189

Report of the Special Rapporteur on Violence Against Women, Its Causes and Consequences On Online Violence Against Women and Girls from a Human Rights Perspective, [18 June 2018], A/HRC/38/47

Karl Ricanek Jr. and Chris Boehnen, 'Facial Analytics: From Big Data To Law Enforcement,' accessed, Internet 13 July 2019, https://www.researchgate.net/publication/25801914, Doi: 10.1109/MC.2012.308

Evelyn Rose, 'A Feminist Reconceptualisation of Intimate Partner Violence Against Women: A Crime Against Humanity and a State Crime,' [2015] 53 Women's Studies International Forum 31-42

Jeanne Sarson and Linda MacDonald, 'Global NST Categories in the Private/Domestic Sphere,' Accessed Internet 28 June 2019 at http://nonstatetorture.org/~nonstate/what-is-nst/non-state-torture

Jeanne Sarson and Linda MacDonald, 'Having Non-State Torture Recognized by the UN and Member States as an Infringement of Women's Human Rights is Imperative,' [2018] 33(1 & 2) Canadian Woman Studies/Les Cahrers De La Femme 144

Jeanne Sarson and Linda MacDonald, 'The Non-State Torture (NST) Wheel: A Fact Sheet,' Accessed Internet 28 June 2019 at http://nonstatetorture.org/~nonstate/application/files/7415/3694/3648/NSTwheelFACTSHEETkeepv2.pdf

Matthew Saul, 'Identifying Jus Cogens Norms: The Interaction of Scholars And International Judges' (May 2014) Asian Journal of International Law, 1

Matthew Robert Shillito, 'Untangling the "Dark Web": An Emerging Technological Challenge for the Criminal Law,' [2019] 28:2 Infor. & Communications Tech. L. 186

Alexander Shytov, 'Indecency on the Internet and International Law,' [2005] 13(2) Int'l J. of Law and Inform. Tech., 260-280

Dubravka Simonovic, 'Global and Regional Standards on Violence Against Women: The Evolution and Synergy of the CEDAW and Istanbul Conventions,' [2014] 36(3) Human Rights Quarterly 590

Malgorzata Skorzewska-Amberg, Pornography in Cyberspace-European Regulations,' [2011] 5(2) Masaryk U. J. of L. and Tech. 261

Lorena Sosa, *Intersectionality In the Human Rights Legal Framework On Violence Against Women: At the Centre Or The Margins?* [2017] Cambridge, UK, Cambridge University Press

Nicolas Suzor, Bryony Seignior, and Jennifer Singleton, 'Non-Consensual Porn and the Responsibilities of Online Intermediaries,' [2017] 40 Melbourne U. L. R. 1057

Brooke Stedman, 'The Leap from Theory to Practice: Snapshot of Women's Rights Through A Legal Lens,' [2013] 29(77) Merkourios 4

Graham Templeton, 'The FBI's Largest Ever Blow to Child Porn and the Deep Web, and Its Possible Ripple Effects,' [5 August 2013] Extremetech.com

Hugh Thirlway, 'International Law and Practice: Human Rights in Customary Law: An Attempt to Define Some Issues,' [2015] 28 Leiden J. of Int'l Law 495

Bruce Garreth Westlake and Richard Frank, 'Seeing the Forest Through the Trees: Identifying Key Players in the Online Distribution of Child Sexual Exploitation Material,' [December 2016] accessed, Internet 13 July 2019, https://www.researchgate.net/publication/332234126

Austin Vining, 'No Means No: An Argument for the Expansion of the Rape Shield Laws to Cases of Nonconsensual Pornography,' [2019] 25 Wm. & Mary J. Race Gender & Soc. Just. 303

Keith D. Watson, 'The Tor Network: A Global Inquiry Into the Legal Status of Anonymity Networks,' [2012] 11 Wash. U. Global Stud. L. Rev. 715

Thomas Weatherall, Jus Cogens International Law and Social Contract. (2015, 2017) Cambridge University Press

Ryan White, Puneet V. Kakkar and Vicki Chou, 'Prosecuting Darknet Marketplaces: Challenges and Approaches,' [2019] 67 U.S. Att'ys Bull. 65

Yukino Yamamoto, Caroline Norma, and Ruwan Dep Weerasinghe, 'Consumer Involvement in Japanese Pornography Productions,' [2018] 3(2) Dignity: A J. on Sexual Exploitation and Violence 1

Matt Zapotosky, 'Justice Department Announces Takedown of AlphaBay, A Dark Web Marketplace For Drugs and Other Illicit Goods; Attorney General Jeff Sessions Called the Case the "Largest Dark Web Takedown In World History"' [20 July 2017] Washington Post Blogs

About Author Sara Johann

Sara Johann, J.D., M.A., M.S. has written twelve books including novels and law books. The author lives in London, England where she is obtaining an LLM in International Human Rights Law at the University of London. She has lived in Rome, Italy, and the United States. Her background is in law, theology, politics, human rights, and forensic psychology. Johann is also an artist and photographer. Contact Sara Johann at saraljohann@gmail.com. You can learn more about her and find links to her websites at https://www.linkedin.com/in/sara-johann-499aa324/

www.ingramcontent.com/pod-product-compliance
Lightning Source LLC
Chambersburg PA
CBHW021421210526
45463CB00001B/477